Unique times call for unique strategies and within Dave's book, you will find the hidden wealth many of us have been passing up all along. As a financial professional, we help clients break free of outdated financial wisdom and redefine how a mortgage can actually be a springboard towards reaching financial goals. Thank you Dave for providing an extremely helpful resource that will enhance our process!

-Matthew Sapaula, President, Matthew Sapaula, Inc, IL

Folks going through divorce or other break-ups often need to be educated on a variety of subjects. This book is a must read for those encountering real estate/mortgage transactions. This book is a great resource to recommend to my clients to help them make the right choice with their finances.

-Jamie K. Von Ellen, Esq., Wolkstein, Von Ellen & Brown, LLC, NJ

In today's treacherous economy, with falling real estate values, tightening credit and a shrinking job market, home owners of all kinds need to take a fresh look at how they are using their home and their mortgages. This is true for first time home buyers as well as for long time home owners. Most people fail to pay adequate attention to the type, length and terms of their mortgages. In today's real estate market being so cavalier can mean real personal disaster. Dave Muti's book (Mortgages: What YOU Need to Know) is perhaps the single most important resource available on today's mortgage market. It's the one book you can turn to for <u>all</u> of the mortgage related information you need to make smart, informed decision that will impact you and your family for years to come.

-Jack Killion, Adjunct Professor, Fairleigh Dickinson University School of Business, Managing Partner, Eagle Rock Diversified Fund, LP, a fund of hedge funds, NJ

As a financial planner this book has become an essential first step in having our clients understand how critical their mortgage is to their overall financial well being. We give this book out to all our clients at our initial consultation. It helps clients understand how their mortgage fits into their overall financial picture and how it affects the funding of their retirement assets.

-Christopher J. Lester, President, Professional Planning Services, NJ

MORTGAGES:
WHAT YOU NEED TO KNOW

Strategies to Take Control of Your Financial Future

Dave Muti

Pocket Guide Press

Disclaimer

The materials presented in this book are accurate and presented to the best of the author's knowledge. The information is not meant to provide legal, financial and/or tax advice and readers are encouraged to do their own due diligence to verify the information as it applies to them as laws often change and can vary state by state. All references to interest rates and any projected rates of return are simply examples for illustration purposes. Rates change frequently and depending upon when one reads the book, they can be higher or lower, although the underlying principals will still apply. Any and all projections and illustrations are not meant to be relied on as performance data, and projections may be impacted by changes in the law. Relevance of some principles may change or become incorrect based upon changes in the law. Neither the author nor publisher assumes any liability for any losses that may be incurred or allegedly incurred directly or indirectly by actions taken by readers based upon the information herein. Any and all liability or alleged liability is expressly disclaimed. All stories and client case studies are based on true events but the names have been changed to protect identities. The information in this book should not be considered as a solicitation for services.

If you would like to purchase this book by the case for use in educational workshops, sales training or simply for distribution to your clients, please visit www.mortgageswhatyouneedtoknow.com for more details and special pricing.

If you would like to hire the author for speaking engagements and/or training events for your staff, sales force or continuing education credits please send an email to speak@ mortgageswhatyouneedtoknow.com. Suggested audiences are corporate real estate offices, corporate mortgage offices, family law/divorce and real estate sections of bar associations, college finance courses, credit counseling and Financial Planning and CPA associations.

Cover by Jen Huppert Design
Book layout by The Carey Group, LLC

ISBN-13: 978-0-9816698-0-9
ISBN-10: 0-9816698-0-8

— To Colleen, David, Jr., and Charlie

HOW TO USE THIS BOOK

This book is a step by step guide on how to improve and take control of your financial future. Each chapter builds on another and there are many suggestions for you to implement immediately. At the end there is a resources section that tells you where to find much of the specific information I refer to throughout the book, as well as a link to my website. This will enable you to get the forms referred to for free so you don't have to re-create or photocopy them.

Acknowledgments

My heartfelt thanks to my wife Colleen and my sons David, Jr. and Charlie, who allowed me time on Sunday mornings to go to the office to have the peace and quiet needed to write this book. If not for their patience and love I never would have been able to complete it.

I would like to thank my production assistant Mara Morris for her help, and for generally putting up with me in the office. I am grateful to my colleague Spence Killam, whom I relied on for some of the finer points and to my sister-in-law Diana O'Dowd for proofing my writings and to my editor Carla Main who gave this book its professional touch. A special thanks to all of my clients. If not for their need for information I would not have thought to write this book nor had the stories from which to draw. Lastly, thanks to you, the reader. Hopefully the information contained in this book will provide you with the knowledge you need for a brighter future.

Table of Contents

INTRODUCTION

MORTGAGES: WHAT YOU NEED TO KNOW

If you already have a mortgage do you need to read this book? That's a fair question. This book is for:

- ✓ People who have a mortgage and feel they need to refinance
- ✓ People who have a mortgage and might move, necessitating a new mortgage
- ✓ People who have a mortgage and might buy a vacation home in the future, necessitating a mortgage
- ✓ People who don't own a home and hope to buy one some day
- ✓ People who have a mortgage and are not sure whether they should refinance
- ✓ People who want to learn more about how to manage their mortgage and their finances in general
- ✓ Financial advisors wanting to learn more and offer this as a resource to their clients
- ✓ Realtors that want to better understand financing as well as provide a copy to their clients as a resource
- ✓ Loan officers looking grow their advisory role

- ✓ Divorce attorney's to better assist their clients who want to better understand a mortgage and their finances

A mortgage is the most important financial decision (and usually the biggest) that most Americans will ever make. The type of mortgage you choose will have a direct impact on when you can retire and with how much. Whether you bought this book because you are contemplating buying your first house or you are a seasoned real estate investor, you will walk away with knowledge that you can start to use right away.

My inspiration to write this came from my clients as well as the financial planners, certified public accountants and attorneys with whom I work. I have found over the years that although most people know what a mortgage is, they do not really know the different types, and how they work. Moreover, once the mortgage is taken out, it is important to have the necessary knowledge as to the steps needed to improve both your short- and long-term financial outlook.

The ultimate goal of this book is to educate you, the consumer, so when it comes time to choose a mortgage you will be empowered to make the right choice and to take responsibility for your actions. Especially in light of today's headlines, consumers need to be aware of the different types of mortgages. More importantly, consumers should be aware of the right questions to ask the mortgage broker or banker. Don't just follow what the talking heads on TV recommend.

I will uncover the common mistakes people make with mortgages and explain how different programs affect you. *Mortgages: What You Need to Know* takes a complicated subject and breaks it down into easy to understand chapters that build upon each other. I am confident that once you have finished reading this book you will have a better understanding of mortgages and how they can help you take control of your financial future. Enjoy!

Chapter One

Know Thy Credit Score

79% of all credit reports contain some type of error.
~National Association of State Public Interest Research Groups

Regard your good name as the richest jewel you can possibly be possessed of— for credit is like fire; when once you have kindled it you may easily preserve it, but if you once extinguish it, you will find it an arduous task to rekindle it again.
~Socrates, Greek Philosopher, 469 - 399 BC

Benjamin Franklin once said "credit is money". Although both he and Socrates were referring to having credit for purchasing goods, their words still ring true today. Whether renting a new apartment, applying for a credit card, a mortgage or even homeowner's insurance (yes, homeowner's insurance!), your credit score will determine the interest rate or premium you are quoted. In essence your credit score has become the filter many industries use to decide whether they want to do business with you and at what price.

In this chapter I will explain:

- What a credit score is;
- What a credit score is based on;
- How a credit score should be maintained.

The most common credit score used and talked about is the FICO score, created by the Fair Isaac Corporation. It is the standard for the mortgage industry as well as many others, and it can range from a low of 350 to a high of 850.[1] The higher the score, the lower the interest rate you will be offered, potentially saving you hundreds if not thousands of dollars a year. The magic number you want to remain above is 720; about half of the country maintains a score above this number.

As you begin to move below 720, interest rates may begin to rise. Fall below 500 and you may not be able to take out a mortgage. This is the case *even if you currently have a mortgage.* How the FICO score is determined is one of the most common questions we hear from clients trying to improve their credit score. While the exact formulas used by the three biggest credit agencies that utilize FICO's standard of scoring are a well guarded industry secret, as mortgage planners we do know the following.

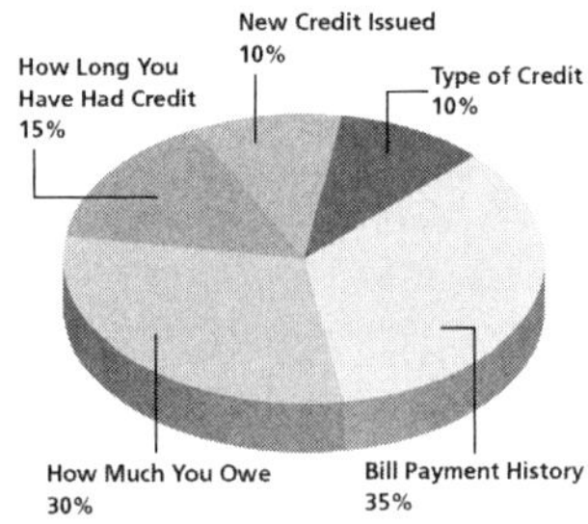

Are All Late Payments Equal?

Your credit score is largely determined by your relationship with creditors, past and present. Your payment history, or how you pay your bills, makes up 35% of your score. How much you owe is 30% and how long you have had credit is

[1] As of the time this book went to press, the industry indicated a new scoring model that will become the standard. Although the numbers will change under the new model, the principals in this chapter will still apply.

another 15%. The type of credit you have and any new credit issued make up 10% each. Factors that are NOT considered in this formula are your income, savings, age, race, geographic location or marital status. ***Basically the score indicates your track record of making payments to companies to which you owe money including your utility bills***. Although it seems as though the agencies should use an exact formula, knowing what affects each component it is more of an art form than a science.

The formulas are proprietary to each of the agencies that rate your credit; they do not have to disclose how they come up with their final number.[2] Nonetheless, experience in reading credit reports provides long-time mortgage planners with what we think affects your score on a daily basis. The largest factor is the category of "paying your bills on time." While it is best to always pay your bills on or before the date that they are due, paying a bill a few days late and incurring a late charge will not necessarily go on your credit report. Having a "late" on your credit report means the specific account is 30 days or more past its due date. The more "lates" you have, the lower your score will go. If you have a bill that is 60, 90 or even 120 days late your score will rapidly decrease. But even if you already have a "late" on your report, the more time that elapses between the date you were late and the present date, the more your score will improve.

The mortgage industry has two major thresholds when looking at any late payments on your report:

- Are the late payments older than **12** months?; and
- Are the late payments older than **24** months?

Each milestone will provide you with better financing solutions as your late payments fade with time. In addition, a mortgage "late" is much more serious than a credit card "late".

[2] The three agencies most commonly used by the mortgage industry are Equifax/Beacon, Transunion and Experian.

So if it comes down to a choice of "which bill to pay" *always* choose your mortgage payment and never miss paying it. The consequences of missing a mortgage payment are far too great. A mortgage is typically a person's largest debt. Moreover, the higher the interest rate, the more it costs you.

Types Of Debt, Credit History

How much you owe combined with what types of credit you have available make up the "art" side of the calculation in evaluating a credit report. You might think that if you owe less you will have a better score. Unfortunately that is not always true. This portion of your score is determined by a delicate three-way dance between your types of credit (mortgage, car loans and credit cards), how much you owe, and how much credit you have available to you. Having too many credit cards can be a negative and so can having only one. Having a credit card with a high limit can be a good thing, as long as you are not near that limit. The same rule applies with a second mortgage or a home equity line of credit. When you have lots of credit available you want to make sure you "use" that credit but do not maintain a high balance. The closer your balance is to the maximum credit available to you, the lower your score will go.

The last two components of your score are the length of your credit history and new accounts. Of course the longer you have credit history the longer your track record will be. However, another important factor is how long you have had a particular account. The longer a particular account is open and active the better your score will be, assuming of course there are no "lates" on that account. Opening up a bunch of new accounts and playing the credit card "balance-switching" game does not look good to the agencies.

Now you know what a FICO score is and how it is calculated. The big question is: how do you maintain a good score?

As the saying goes, most people don't plan to fail, they simply fail to plan. It happens all too often in our business. But if clients regularly monitored their credit scores we would be able to save them thousands of dollars on their mortgages. This is essential: if you are *planning* to buy a home, don't just go and look at houses, make an offer and then get a mortgage. You may not like what you are offered as a result of your FICO score. My suggestion is to plan ahead for this event. The same holds true if you are thinking about refinancing.

Improving your credit score is kind of like getting ready to run a marathon. You can't just sign up today and expect to run tomorrow.

If you have a poor credit history or if there is inaccurate information on your report it can take *months* to repair and correct. I have a saying that we have been using for years, *Make Life Happen!* Don't sit back and let life happen to you. Being proactive with your credit scores (like with many other areas of your life) will improve the results and your experiences.

It Won't Happen To Me

Some of you reading this may think you don't have to worry about a bad FICO score because you have never missed a payment and you have excellent credit. Well, so thought one of my clients when he called me to get a loan for a condo he was buying.

This client, we will call him Mark, was referred to us by his attorney and he was only 30 days away from his purchase closing date. Mark advised us that his credit was perfect. However, when we ran it as part of his application, it turned out that it was not. One of the student loans that Mark co-signed on behalf of his daughter indicated several missed payments despite the fact she was still in school and the first payment was not due for another two years. We still got the mortgage approved at a rate and payment Mark could live with but had Mark proactively monitored his credit scores both his interest rate and payment would have been better. Mark did contact the student loan provider and they agreed that it was a mistake but the damage was done. It took six months to finally reflect the corrected information on his report and at that point it was too late to affect that particular mortgage.

In that example "life happened to Mark" and had he been proactive about checking his credit score he would have been better off. This is not a hard thing to do—it is just like going to the gym, you have to do it regularly. While I am not suggesting that you monitor your scores daily or even weekly, I am suggesting that you institute a bi-annual credit review to ensure your credit is the best it can be so you are not caught off guard like Mark.

If you would like to read in greater depth about the information you need in order to take control of your finances, go to www.MyFICO.com and download a free 20-page booklet entitled *Understanding Your FICO Score*. The site also has a paid service to alert you anytime there is a change to your score and/or credit history. I personally use this service and it is nice to receive an email alert when my score goes up or down and if a new account is opened. In today's world of identity theft this could prove to be a prudent investment. Not only will you save money by ensuring you have good credit but you may be able to prevent any fraudulent charges against your name as well as the accruing interest and legal fees should you become an unfortunate victim. You can also obtain a free credit report from www.annualcreditreport.com, or visit www.lifelock.com for a service that guarantees your good name and credit. If you really want to ensure no one steals your identity, Life Lock will back their service for up to $1,000,000 if your identity is misused while you are their client. If you have ever experienced identity theft, you know how valuable such a guarantee can be.

Make Life Happen! Monitor your credit twice a year. You will be happy you did.

Chapter Two

Trigger Lists

You apply for a mortgage. A couple of weeks later you start to receive numerous phone calls from people you do not know saying that they have your application, have approved you for a loan, or are ready to offer you a lower interest rate. You don't know who they are or how they got your name or how they even know you have applied for a mortgage.

What is going on?

When you began your mortgage application process, you authorized the person you are working with to obtain a mortgage to check your credit.

Then, unbeknownst to you (and even most people in the industry), the next morning the three national credit reporting agencies compile a "trigger list." This list is comprised of consumers who, like you, had their credit pulled in the previous 24 hours while shopping for a mortgage. A similar list is compiled of people who had their credit checked as part of obtaining a new credit card. These trigger lists are then purchased by lenders and firms who sell leads to credit card and mortgage companies based upon the type of firm that ran your credit.

This practice smacks of invasion of privacy and unfair market practices, and would seem to be a violation of the Fair Credit Reporting Act. Unfortunately this practice, known as prescreening, is legal. In fact, several of the largest lenders in the country provide the list of their existing clients to the national credit reporting agencies so when an existing customer of theirs has their credit run by another mortgage company, they are alerted. Then they try and call you to see if they can offer you a "better" deal.

How To Protect Yourself

The important issue for now is to better protect your privacy and stop this from happening to you. If you do not want solicitations, junk mail and phone calls, you need to opt out of having your name reported on these pre-screened trigger lists. You can do this electronically for five years or sign up permanently by requesting removal from these lists in writing. To accomplish this, as well as eliminate most of the junk mail that comes from these target lists (which are full of your personal information), call 1-800-5-OPTOUT (1-888-567-8688) or log on to www.optoutprescreen.com. By getting off of these lists you will have less of your information floating out there, which in turn will limit your chances of having your identity stolen.

If you decide to opt out from these trigger lists you will need to provide your name, address, home phone number and social security number. This process is completely confidential and if you use the website it is a safe and encrypted site provided by the national consumer reporting agencies as required by Federal law.

Additional resources about the opt-out process can be found at The Federal Trade Commission's Prescreening Information Pamphlet at the following URL:
www.ftc.gov/bcp/conline/pubs/credit/prescreen.pdf.

Don't wait. Take this book over to your computer now, type in the URLs shown above and remove your name from these lists!

Chapter Three

Types of Mortgages

The type of mortgage you choose will directly impact your ability to retire.

That is a bold statement but as you read through this book you will see my basis for making it. Unlike past generations, today you have many options when trying to decide on a mortgage for your home. As recently as the mid-90s, we only had a handful of types of mortgages. Today, if you can dream one up, the type of mortgage you want probably exists.

This chapter explains the different types of mortgages as well as their different working components so you have a better understanding of them. However, before we begin looking at the available programs we need to understand how life today is different than it was for our parents and grandparents. How do the changes in living habits affect your mortgage and financial well being? This is the cornerstone to determining the type of mortgage that may be right for you.

Today we live the I-have-to-have-it-now lifestyle while trying to keep up with the Joneses. This could be one reason why the national average for owning a home is roughly seven years and the typical mortgage lasts roughly 4.2 years. It could also explain why the average household has in excess of $25,000 in credit card debt and less than $27,000 set aside in retirement accounts. Prior generations had a more stable lifestyle of one job, a pension, one house and one mortgage.

Today, pension plans seem to be a thing of the past and most Americans will hold five or more jobs throughout their careers. Furthermore, my professional experience indicates that most of us will have at least four homes throughout our adult lives: a starter home; a move-up home (both of which will last three to seven years); a dream home that we will live in the longest through much of our working career and while the kids get through college (some people have several dream homes as their lifestyle and finances change). And finally, we downsize to a smaller home as empty nesters or simply to enjoy a better retirement. So depending upon the stage of life you are in, you should choose a mortgage that best suits your situation while maximizing your cash flow, taking both your short- and long-term financial goals into consideration.

With each type of mortgage there are advantages and disadvantages as well as many different options. Your mortgage planner should explain them in consultation with you so together you can choose the appropriate program. Before any program can be recommended, a comprehensive discovery session *must* be completed to fully understand the circumstances and goals of each client. Your doctor does not prescribe medicine for you until he asks you a lot of questions, runs some tests, and reviews the diagnosis with you and his recommended treatment. A good mortgage planner will do the same with you and your finances. While you will not directly die from having the wrong type of mortgage, the stress brought on by financial difficulties could send you to the doctor.

The Two Basic Mortgage Types

Basically there are two main categories of mortgages: amortized mortgages and interest only mortgages. Then within these two categories there are several types which function the same way and are referred to by the same name. The distinguishing factor between them is whether the debt is amortized (that is, paid down), or whether only interest is paid.

Another distinguishing factor is whether the loan is conforming or jumbo.[3] The information provided here should give you a better understanding of the choices you have today, though it is not meant to be comprehensive.

An **amortized** loan means that your monthly payment is comprised of both principal and interest. Initially the vast majority of the payment is interest while a small portion goes towards paying down the balance of the loan. Fifteen years into a 30-year fixed rate mortgage you would still have more than 71% of the original balance remaining.

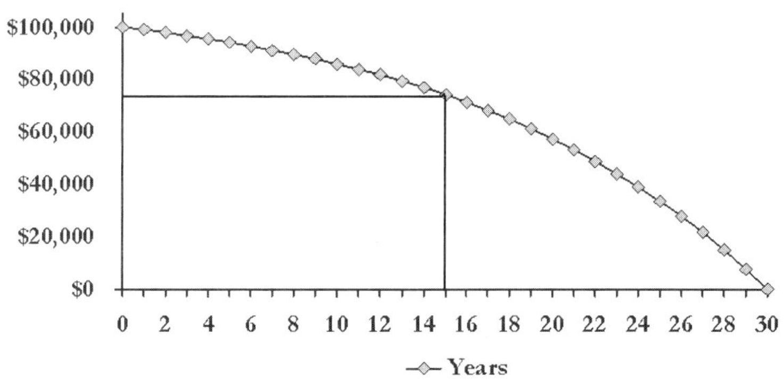

If you remain in this loan for its entire life, the principal component of your monthly payment really begins to increase in the second half of the term while the interest portion decreases. The chart on the next page illustrates what the payments would look like for a $100,000 30-year fixed rate mortgage at 6.5% where the total payment would be $632.07. The illustrated payments are for the first payment at the beginning of each five year period.

[3] A conforming mortgage may be issued at or below the amount set for jumbo loan programs. As of the date of writing, conforming programs were set at $417,000 or below. Loans above $417,000 are jumbo loans.

Payment	Principal	Interest	Balance
1	$90.40	$541.67	$99,909.60
61	$125.01	$507.06	$93,485.83
121	$172.87	$459.20	$84,602.93
181	$239.04	$393.03	$72,319.50
241	$330.55	$301.52	$55,333.76
301	$457.10	$174.97	$31,845.58
360	$628.68	$3.39	($2.19)

As you can see, at the 181st payment (which would be after 15 years) you still have $72,319.50 remaining and only 38% of your total payment is comprised of principal. The same chart and schedule would be used when calculating an adjustable rate mortgage that is amortizing for the fixed portion of the loan as detailed below.

Interest Only loans are exactly what they sound like. Your monthly payments consist only of the interest portion of the money borrowed. In essence, you are only paying for the "cost" of the money and nothing towards the principal. You do have the option of sending in principal payments but they are not required. Interest Only loans may be the best use of your cash flow in conjunction with a comprehensive mortgage plan. These types of loans are typically used in Cash Management Strategies to build long term wealth. The big pro of these mortgages is that your payment will be lower than with other types. One of the cons, as often argued by the mainstream media, is that you are not paying down any principal on your mortgage. However, you always have the option of paying principal any time you want; it is just not part of your regularly scheduled payment. Chapter Nine is dedicated to this type of mortgage and I will expand in that chapter on how to use the Interest Only mortgage to your advantage.

Fixed Rate mortgages will have a fixed percentage rate and a fixed monthly payment for a certain number of years. The longer ones will carry higher rates than other types of mortgages but they offer the security and certainty of knowing your monthly payment and interest rate will not change for the term of the loan. The most common are 30- and 15-year fixed rate mortgages.

Ten-year and 20-year fixed rate mortgages have been around for a while and recently 40-year and even 50-year fixed rate mortgages have become available. However, the longer term mortgages sometimes work slightly differently; after the initial 30 years there *may* be a balloon payment (see below) rather than a true amortization schedule over 40 years. The longer term of 40 years will be used to calculate your monthly payment, which will be lower than a 30-year fixed rate, but if you remain in the loan for longer than thirty years you may have a lump sum payment due at the end of the 30th year.

Arms, Balloons And More

Adjustable Rate Mortgages (ARMs) have an interest rate that will adjust over time and monthly payments that are recalculated on a scheduled basis to reflect changes in the market interest rate. They apply to both amortized and interest only programs. Interest rates for ARMs are typically lower than the rates one finds in fixed-rate mortgages. ARMs allow you to fix the interest rate for the length of time that you plan to hold the loan without paying a higher cost for interest rate protection during a time when you will not need it. When you know *for certain* that you will only have a particular mortgage for a certain number of years these types of loans are the best choice. Chapter Eight is dedicated in detail to this type of mortgage and how they work.

Balloon mortgages are really a subset of fixed rate mortgages for a limited number of years with one big difference. The big difference here is when the initial period expires the *entire balance* of the loan becomes due. In other words, you must pay back the remaining loan balance at the conclusion of the initial term. This is usually accomplished either by refinancing your loan or selling the property. An example would be a seven-year balloon. The payment will be calculated on a 30-year amortized schedule but the loan is due in full at the end of the seventh year.

Option ARMs are very complicated mortgages and should only be used by financially savvy clients. They are often referred to as Cash Flow Mortgages, Pick-A-Payment Mortgage and Negative Amortization Loans. Though not for the average consumer, this type of mortgage can be the best financial tool available when used correctly to manage cash flow and re-direct monthly expenditures towards retirement, college planning and long term wealth building. Option ARMs were designed for higher income earners who desire the flexibility of making the minimum payments to free up cash for other investments. There are also a limited number of reasons to use them for certain goal-oriented transactions, but they should be used with caution and in consultation with your mortgage planner. Too many mortgage companies advertise a low rate and low payment and misuse Option ARM mortgages to lure people into buying a house they really cannot afford.

Make no mistake about it, no matter what anyone tells you, with an Option ARM mortgage your loan balance will ***increase*** each month if you make only the minimum payment.[4] In other words, if you make no more than the minimum payment every month, your mortgage loan balance will go *up*. Option ARMs seem complicated at first but a qualified mortgage planner should be able to break them down into pieces that are easily understandable.

Basically, an Option ARM provides you with up to four payment options to choose from each month, and each one usually has a higher monthly payment as you move down the list. The four options are:

1. Minimum payment option: This is a discounted payment that is typically less than the interest-only

[4] An exception was the period of historically low interest rates in 2002 to 2004.

payment. By making this payment your loan balance will increase each month, meaning it is negatively amortizing. In other words, rather than the loan balance decreasing, the loan balance will increase or "negatively amortize." This minimum payment adjusts yearly and it (not the rate) usually will increase by 7.5% each year.

2. Interest-Only Payment Option (if available). The interest rate for this option will adjust monthly.
3. Fully amortized 30-year payment option. The interest rate for this option will adjust monthly.
4. Fully amortized 15-year payment option. The interest rate for this option will adjust monthly.

	Loan Amount	Interest Rate	Term	Payment	
1	$100,000.00	1.250%	-	$333.25	
*Represents deferred interest **if** you choose the minimum payment*					-$225.08
2	$100,000.00	6.700%	-	$558.33	none
3	$100,000.00	6.700%	30	$645.28	none
4	$100,000.00	6.700%	15	$882.14	none

Projected Increase of Minimum Monthly Payments	
year 2	$358.25
year 3	$385.11
year 4	$414.00
year 5	$445.05

As you can see, if you choose to make the minimum payment your loan balance will *increase* by $225.08 each month and your payments will increase each year. There are limitations to how much this can increase and how the minimum payment gets recalculated each year. So be sure to ask your mortgage planner to detail what the projected minimum payments will be, as well as how much would be deferred each year. There are many moving parts to this type of mortgage and the brief overview given here provides you with just enough information to be able to speak intelligently with your mortgage planner should this type of mortgage interest you. Visit www.mortgageswhatyouneedtoknow.com for a calculator you can use to illustrate your situation as well as obtain a free report providing more details for this type of loan.

Areas For A Narrow Audience

Reverse mortgages are generally reserved for a very small segment of our society. In my opinion this group is made up of less than 5% of people over the age of 72. With this type of loan, instead of making payments to the bank, they pay you. Depending upon the type of program, you can elect to receive monthly payments or a lump sum distribution of your equity. Since it is technically a loan of your own money, there is no income tax due on the money you receive.

Reverse mortgages only make sense for a very small percentage of the population. The loans involve large up-front fees and often higher interest rates compared with other types of mortgages. The amount of money you can borrow will often be much less than the equity you have in your home as it may be limited based upon FHA guidelines and your age. Another reason I don't like these mortgages is because, depending upon a person's circumstances, there are usually other choices that make more sense. However, if you have a house that is paid in full (or close to it), you have no other money, your income is limited to social security and you are not able to work, a reverse mortgage may prove to be your best alternative.

Lastly, although they fit into the types of mortgages detailed in this chapter, I felt the need to call out two additional programs called **FHA** (Federal Housing Administration) and **VA** (Veterans Administration) mortgages. Both of these programs are backed by the federal government and they offer fixed rate and ARM choices. These can be good programs for people who have less than perfect credit as well as a host of other reasons. I am not detailing anything further here because, at the end of the day, they are just like any other loan once you have it. At the end of the day these loans fall into the categories of fixed rate or ARMs but you will not have an interest only option. If you think you can benefit from one of these programs ask your mortgage planner. Likewise, I am not detailing programs such as "first time home buyer" and "high net worth individuals."

CHAPTER FOUR

KNOW HOW MUCH YOU CAN AFFORD

The cost of the house you want and the amount lenders will lend to you may be completely different. They may be willing to lend you more than you desire. Or perhaps you want to buy more house than you can pay for. Either way, your "DTI" ratios (explained below) will determine your buying power. Here is what you need to do to prepare for that event.

After you decide that you want to buy a house, the next decision you have to make is how much you can afford. If you already own a home and want to refinance in order to consolidate debts, then this is a key question for you. While your circumstances may be different from someone else's, the formulas used in this chapter are applicable for all mortgages. You should understand what the lenders look at as well as your comfort level based upon your financial blueprint.

These formulas will determine what neighborhood you can afford to live in and whether you will be buying at the high or low end of that neighborhood. Keep in mind that most people end up shooting too high and buying a house that is a stretch for them. This is why many people today find themselves financially strapped. Even if you qualify to buy a bigger home, you need to look closely at your overall financial goals to ensure that you are not buying beyond your means. A qualified mortgage planner will be able to help you determine this and set a plan in motion to achieve your goals of homeownership as well as financial security.

My suggestion is that you buy at the low- to mid-level range of any neighborhood. This will provide you with more buyers when the time comes to sell as well as room to increase your home's value by making improvements. If you buy the most expensive home on the block you really don't have anything to aspire to. Moreover, the potential to increase the value of your home through improvements and appreciation will not be as great as it would be with other homes.

As with many facets of our industry, the answer to "how much can you afford" has more than one determining factor. The starting point comes down to your *total* household income. When applying for a mortgage, your mortgage planner will want to know the sources of all your income. Do not leave anything out. If you have a part time business selling cookware or candles to make extra money, tell your lender about it. Don't assume anything and let your mortgage planner look at your entire picture. The important thing is that you completely disclose everything to your mortgage planner and provide him or her with all documents they request. Doing this up front will take the guess work out of the equation and allow your mortgage planner to properly advise you on your anticipated purchase or refinance as well as long term planning.

Say you have decided to buy a house and you have picked out a mortgage planner to work with. When you meet, he or she will ask you for your tax returns, W-2s, pay-stubs and bank statements. With this information the planner will be able to provide you with that all important pre-qualification letter, which is an estimate of your buying power. The pre-qualification letter is something that realtors will request before they begin showing you houses. The more complete the information provided, the more accurate your qualification will be. Consequently, you can be more confident that once the loan is submitted, you will get the loan approval to buy the house you want.

CRUNCHING THE NUMBERS

Once you have gathered the information your mortgage planner needs, ask yourself what you *think* you can afford. This question serves two purposes: first it gives the mortgage planner a starting point, and second it helps you better understand what you are looking for.

Your mortgage planner will want to look at all of your tax returns and pay-stubs to determine your *gross* monthly income. The lenders will look at your gross income and not your take home pay because the amount you take home may change once you become a homeowner and have tax deductible mortgage interest. Your mortgage planner will also ask you what you think the property taxes will be for the house you want to buy. He or she will then come up with an estimate for homeowner's insurance and begin to look at mortgage programs. The reason all of this information is important is that it is used to determine what your **D**ebt-**T**o-**I**ncome ratios are. We refer to this as DTIs and there are two types: the "front ratio" and the "back ratio".

The front DTI ratio consists of your total housing expenses on a refinance, or your anticipated housing expenses on a purchase, divided by your gross income. The traditional range of this front DTI ratio is between 28 and 33 depending upon the ultimate lender, as each one has different guidelines. If you are below this level (which you should be) then you will most likely receive an approval from the lender as long as your back ratio is also acceptable and you meet all of the other guidelines that lender may have. Your mortgage planner will be able to counsel you on this.

To determine your front DTI ratio your mortgage planner will run the following calculation.

Front DTI Ratio Calculation:

Monthly mortgage payment + Monthly property taxes + Monthly cost of homeowner's insurance Gross monthly income	=	front DTI ratio

Let's plug in some numbers to see what this might look like for you:

$1,875	mortgage payment		
+ $800	monthly property taxes	=	28.6 front ratio
+ $70	monthly cost of homeowners insurance		
$9,583.33	average monthly income		

We arrived at your average monthly income by taking your total gross annual income and dividing it by 12. We do not use your last pay-stub to determine this as it might be larger or smaller than average depending upon overtime, commissions, bonuses or other factors. In this illustration we used $115,000 as the total household income from all sources. Divided by 12, it yields an average monthly income of $9,583.33. Simplifying the formula, the front DTI calculation looks like this:

> $2,745 total housing expenses ÷ $9,583.33 average monthly income = 28.6 front ratio

Not to complicate matters, but if you are buying into a condominium complex or if there are any association dues or fees for your home, that monthly amount will also be added to your other monthly housing expenses and the total then divided by your average monthly income.

Now that we know the amount of your front ratio, we need to determine your back ratio. The traditional range of this back DTI ratio is between 33 and 38. Again, this will depend upon the ultimate lender. Some will go even higher, but I recommend that you stay within this range, preferably at the low end so you will have money left over to invest. This back ratio consists of *all* of your monthly expenses as they appear on your credit report or as they appear on your tax returns including any alimony and/or child support payments. Things that would appear in this calculation are car payments, student loans, credit card bills and any other properties you may own as investments or otherwise.

BACK DTI RATIO CALCULATION:

$2,745 total housing expenses
+ $495 car payment = 37.5 back DTI ratio
+ $350 monthly credit card payments
$9,583.33 average monthly income

$3,590 total monthly expenses ÷ $9,583.3 average monthly income = 37.5 back ratio

Now, armed with your DTI ratios, you and your mortgage planner can determine the right loan for your circumstances (see Chapters Five, Six and Seven) and then look at the guidelines that are applicable to that program.

RESERVES

Another main factor that determines the size of the loan you qualify for will be the type of mortgage you are seeking. This may be further limited by your credit, other debts you have, and the amount of reserves you have.

Reserves refer to how much liquid cash you have in the bank or will have left in the bank after your down payment and closing costs. You may use your 401k or other retirement accounts to satisfy this reserve requirement. Some lenders will require a reserve of six months' worth of total housing expenses and others may only require three months' worth in your combined accounts.

No matter the guidelines, my recommendation is that you build up at least six months' worth of all your monthly expenses because you never know what curve ball life may throw. I further suggest that this reserve be in a liquid account like a money market or savings account in addition to your 401k, IRA or other retirement account.

Once your mortgage planner has all of the information, and together you have chosen the right mortgage for your circumstances, you will know your DTI ratios. If you are at the high end or above the suggested range, your mortgage planner will be able to advise you as to whether you qualify for the type of mortgage you prefer. What we suggest to many of our clients is that they reduce their price range and not reach above their means even if we *can* get them approved. By reducing their monthly housing expenses we can provide them with peace of mind as well as more cash to invest toward long term wealth building.

Chapter Five

Down Payment

How much money should you put down when you purchase a home? This is one of the oldest questions faced when purchasing real estate. The rule of thumb has always been to put down 20% of the purchase price if you can. Of course, if you had more available, then you were advised to increase the amount. This chapter will offer a contrarian viewpoint to this established way of thinking. The general principle behind a large down payment is that you will have a smaller mortgage and therefore a smaller mortgage payment. While that may be true, the operative question is: does a large down payment make the *best use of your money*?

In order to address this question, we must first visit a common misconception regarding home equity and its rate of return. No matter how much (or little) equity you have in your house, the rate of return is always the same: zero. This is important to understand because you would not put your hard earned money onto a mutual fund that advertises a 0% rate of return, so why put it into your house? It is dead money that provides the same return as it would if you had literally buried it in your backyard or put it under your mattress.

Now you might think: How is that possible? I put down $100,000 on the purchase of a $500,000 home five years ago and it is now worth $600,000. This is a 100% return on my investment of equity. The common mistake most people make is confusing return on equity with the appreciation of real estate values. True, the house went up in value, but you would have realized this gain regardless of whether you had a mortgage on the property. Indeed, you would have realized it even if you had financed the entire purchase. A home's appreciation in value does not depend upon the size of the down payment. Real estate values go up and down irrespective of the size of down payments and mortgages. Real estate value is a factor of market supply and demand. The analogy is that boats on the bay will rise and fall with the tide no matter how big or small they are.

The chart below provides a clearer explanation as to how this works. To make the math easy to follow, we use an interest-only mortgage in both cases:

	The Smiths	**The Joneses**
Purchase Price	$250,000	$250,000
Down Payment	$200,000	$50,000
Mortgage	$50,000	$200,000
	10 YEARS LATER	
Future Home Value	$411,752	$411,752
Mortgage	$50,000	$200,000
Future Equity	$361,752	$211,752
Less Original Down Payment	$200,000	$50,000
Gain	**$161,752**	**$161,752**

Chart provided by Forgotten Equity, Inc. © 2004 all rights reserved

Here the Smiths and the Joneses each purchase a home. Each family has $200,000 available to use as a down payment. The Smiths decide to follow conventional advice and make a big down payment to reduce their monthly mortgage payments. They only have a $50,000 mortgage. The Joneses on the other hand are privy to the smarter way to purchase their house and they only place $50,000 down. They then invest the remaining

$150,000 they had available in a long term investment account. The illustration further assumes that both houses will appreciate at 5% over the next 10 years and that both families took out interest only mortgages.

TEN YEARS LATER

As you can see, 10 years into the future both homes will appreciate to the same value of $411,752. Remember, the value increases or decreases based upon market demand. It has nothing to do with the size of the mortgage or the amount of equity in a home. If they both then decided to sell, at the closing they would both have the same gain. The Smiths would pay off their mortgage of $50,000 leaving them with $361,752 from which they will deduct their original down payment of $200,000 leaving them with a gain of $161,752. The Joneses on the other hand will pay off their $200,000 mortgage leaving them with $211,752 from which they will deduct their original down payment of $50,000 leaving them with a gain of $161,752.

As counter intuitive as it seems, this illustration proves that regardless of the size of the down payment, the gain is always the difference between the original purchase price and the future value of the home. After 10 years of the home appreciating at a rate of 5% per year, both homes have gained $161,752 in value despite the different down payments. This analysis demonstrates that home equity has a 0% rate of return. Again, you would not put your hard earned money into a mutual fund that advertises a 0% rate of return. Why do the same with down-payment funds?

Now that we have illustrated this critical point, let's get back to the original question: *how much should you put down?* Obviously the smaller the down payment you make, the larger your mortgage and corresponding monthly payments. So I recommend that you take out as large a mortgage as you can *comfortably afford* and place the remaining money you had planned on using as a down payment in an investment account. I am *not* advocating that you buy a bigger house and place less down; I am saying that you should purchase your home within a range that gives you comfortable payments and invest the difference. The actual amount depends upon your household income viewed in respect to how many children you have along with the amount of assets you have earmarked for retirement and how much you contribute to those accounts each month.

Now that we know our equity in the home is not working for us, let's look at investing that down payment somewhere it can. True, this is a book on mortgages. But unless you understand how the money *could* grow, you'd have little incentive to invest it otherwise and would have only part of the tools for creating wealth. If you take only one thing away from this book it should be this: ***The type of mortgage you have dramatically affects your net worth and directly impacts your ability to retire!*** Implementing the strategies outlined in this book through Advanced Mortgage Planning Strategies can help you use your mortgage to create wealth and peace of mind you never thought possible.

Comparing Returns

So let's look back at the Smiths and the Joneses illustration on page 26. Remember: the Joneses were savvy to the strategy of not tying up their money in their house. They invested their $150,000 in an investment account. What type of account to use depends upon personal preference. Since there are countless books written on investing as well as many factors to consider, I will not go into that here.

Now, let's assume that this account is invested tax deferred (or not taxed as earned) and it earns a 7% rate of return. You will have $210,382.76 after five years and $295,072.70 after 10 years. So who would you rather be? The Smiths, who sold their home and walked away with a gain of $161,752 and a net worth of $361,752, or the Joneses, who also walked away with the same gain of $161,752 *plus* an investment account with $295,072 for a total net worth of $506,824. The Joneses, after only

10 years using the strategy of placing less down and investing the difference, created $145,072 more than the Smiths.

If they both decided not to sell and continued along for another 20 years, the Joneses investment account would have grown to $413,854.73 after 15 years, and $1,141,838.26 after 30 years. Meantime, the houses would have appreciated at whatever rate the market dictated. Assuming a modest 5% return over the same time period, the homes would be valued at $319,070 after five years, $407,223 after 10 years, $519,732 after 15 years, and $1,080,485 after 30 years. Now this may seem hard to swallow, but it is simply the power of compounding interest over time. Remember when houses were only $38,000 to $80,000 in the early '70s? So by investing their money separately, the Joneses created an additional $991,838 over 30 years—money that would not have been realized had they done as the Smiths did and placed a larger down payment on their home.

Of course you may think: Hey wait a minute. The Joneses have a bigger mortgage payment. That needs to be factored in. The Joneses' gross payment is larger, but so is the tax deduction they receive from Uncle Sam. While the gross payment might be $750 more per month, assuming a 6% mortgage and a tax bracket of 33%, they would also get a tax savings of $250 each month, so the actual increase in cost is only $500. Even if the Smiths invested that same $500 *each and every month* over the entire 30 years without ever missing a contribution (and what are the chances of that?) their returns would pale in comparison. This $500 per month or $6,000 per year at the same 7% return in a tax deferred account would grow into $36,919.74 after five years, $88,701.60 after 10 years, $161,328.62 after 15 years, and $606,438.25 after 30 years.

Now some of you might say we should run the numbers investing the entire gross difference of $750 each month. Even though it is not a fair comparison, let's take a look at how that would compare. After five years the Smiths would have $55,379.62, after 10 years $133,052.39, after 15 years $241,992.48, and after 30 years $909,657.37. No matter how you compare it, the Joneses still come out ahead since they will have $1,141,838.26 after 30 years. Even if you assume that the Smiths never missed a contribution to their investment account and even taking the full amount between the differences in payments, the Joneses will outpace them by $232,180.88 in this example.

The moral of this chapter: Don't put all of your money down on a house. Invest it in yourself instead and give yourself a chance at creating a retirement.

CHAPTER SIX

THE 10 PERCENT DOWN-PMI DILEMMA

As we covered in the last chapter, the generally accepted rule of thumb when buying a home is putting down at least 20%. Until the run up of real estate values between 2003 and 2006 this was not too difficult for most people. However, with the average sale price across the country at roughly of $300,000, it is getting increasingly harder for many Americans to come up with this magic number of 20%, or $60,000, based upon this average. My mortgage practice is located in Morris County, New Jersey and as of June 2007 the average price was $530,000. You would need to have $106,000 available in cash or as the equity in your current home if you were planning on moving into a bigger home.

That is a lot of money and today's high prices make it very difficult for both first time buyers as well as those who want a nicer home or what I referred to as the "move up" home in Chapter Three. The solution of course is to put less than 20% percent down. However, this raises a new issue: When buying or refinancing a home, if you have less than 20% equity[5] in the home, a lender will require mortgage insurance. So, before we

[5] Equity equals the value of your home or the proposed purchase price less the balance of your mortgage(s) or down payment, as the case may be.

cover the best way to finance your home with less than 20% percent down, we need to define what mortgage insurance is and the length of time lenders require it. Mortgage insurance is a policy for the sole purpose of covering the *lender* should you fail to make payments. It covers the risk for the lender in the event you default on the payments and the lender is forced to foreclose. Its purpose is to make the lender whole so it does not suffer a loss.

Understand this: mortgage insurance does **not** to pay off the loan if you die. That is called life insurance or, a fancier name used by many direct mail solicitors: "mortgage protection insurance."

Now that you understand these basics, let's say you want to put down less than 20%. You have a choice to make: Should you take out two mortgages or one? If you choose to go with one, you then have to decide whether it is better to have one with Private Mortgage Insurance (PMI) or Lender Paid Mortgage Insurance (LPMI). The argument against PMI is that it is not always tax deductible.[6] Therefore, the strategy would be to take out two mortgages so that all payments relating to your mortgages are deductible. You do this by taking out one mortgage for 80% of the purchase price and the other mortgage for 10% or more depending upon how much money you have available to put down on your house.

The requirement to have mortgage insurance is no longer a factor after you build up to 20% or more of equity in your home. This can be accomplished several different ways. One is by paying down your mortgage balance with each payment you make over many years with an amortized mortgage or by paying a lump sum towards the balance of your loan. Another way is waiting for the value of your home to increase (by appreciation of real estate or major home

---

[6] As of January 1, 2007 PMI may be deductible when household income is less than $100,000. Readers should seek the advice of a certified public accountant to see whether they can take advantage of this tax deduction.

improvements) until your loan balance becomes 80% or less of this new value. Of course you can turbo charge both of these methods by making capital improvements to your home.

For the purpose of this chapter we are going to assume that you are buying or refinancing a house valued at $300,000.00. We will detail three different ways to finance this assuming you only have 10% or $30,000 to put down plus a little left over for closing costs and reserves. This means you have to get a mortgage (or mortgages) for the remaining 90% or $270,000.00.

THE LPMI OPTION

Here you would get one loan at 90% with **L**ender **P**aid **M**ortgage **I**nsurance (LPMI). What this means is that the lender takes out the mortgage insurance to cover its loss in the event you default on the payments and it is forced to foreclose on your loan. The lender offsets the cost of the insurance by charging you a higher interest rate on your mortgage. By financing your home this way you can enjoy the full tax deduction of your mortgage payment since there is no separate mortgage insurance payment. While this may seem attractive, this is not always the best option. With LPMI you will be paying an inflated interest rate for the life of your loan. In many cases this period of higher interest will be well beyond the period during which you are actually required to have mortgage insurance, continuing during those years after you have built up the necessary amount of equity.

THE PMI OPTION

Here again you finance the home with one mortgage at 90% in the amount of $270,000 but now you also incur the non-deductible expense *(see footnote on prior page)* of **P**rivate **M**ortgage **I**nsurance (PMI) in the amount of $148.50 per month for this example. This is not always the best solution because this monthly PMI payment is money you are throwing out the window unless you can benefit from the tax deduction. On the other hand, you can do away with the PMI payment once you have achieved 20% of equity of the home's value–assuming you have paid your mortgage on time each and every month. You can gain this equity, as mentioned above, by market appreciation, paying down your mortgage balance and/or perhaps making some improvements to your home.

Let's assume that your $300,000 home appreciates in step with the historical national average of 5% per year. Of course some local markets have appreciated at a higher rate and some at a lower rate but you get the point. In only two and a half years your home would be worth $338,989 which is the amount necessary to have your loan balance equal 80% of your home's value. This also assumes that you had an interest only loan. If you had an amortized loan you would reach this critical point in only two years because you would have paid some of the principal off the balance of your loan. Again, the value of your home may increase faster if you make improvements to your home by updating the kitchen, bathroom, finishing the basement or a host of other ways.

When you reach this point of having at least 20% of equity in your home you can ask your lender (just call the customer service number on your statement) to remove the requirement of your PMI. Upon this request, the lender will ask you to pay for an appraisal which they will order (around $400), to see what your home is now worth. If the value has increased and your loan balance is now only 80% or less of the value of your home, your PMI payment will disappear, providing you with more spendable cash each month. If you currently have PMI and you have been paying for more than two years, you may want to contact your lender to ask about terminating this payment. You might be able to save some money each month! Or better yet, invest that payment towards your retirement.

The Two-Mortgage Option

The last and often the most popular option to finance this transaction would be to take out two mortgages: one at 80%

of the home's value in the amount of $240,000 and the second at 10% in the amount of $30,000. By taking out two mortgages you can avoid the non-deductible cost of insurance if that deduction is not available to you. The rationale behind this strategy is that both mortgages can be deducted on your tax return, therefore making it a better solution. Although you will have two separate mortgage payments to make, the overall cost in some cases will be lower than that for the other options. See chart.

Options detailed with average interest rates		
	LPMI Option	
Loan Amount	rate	mo payment
$270,000.00	7.00%	$1,575.00
	PMI Option	
Loan Amount	rate	mo payment
$270,000.00	6.50%	$1,462.50
Cost of PMI		$148.50
	Total Monthly Payment	$1,611.00
	Two Mortgage Option	
Loan Amounts	rates	mo payment
$240,000.00	6.75%	$1,350.00
$30,000.00	9.25%	$246.80
	Total Monthly Payment	$1,596.80

In this example the better solution is to use the LPMI. However, this may not always the case so make sure when you are applying for your next mortgage that the mortgage planner you are working with is able to review your entire scenario and can make a recommendation that is in your best interest. Ask him or her to provide you with all three different options so you can see the numbers. Don't let the mortgage planner just tell you his or her way is the best way. Ask *why* it is, while taking your short and long term goals into consideration. If the person won't show you, then you should look for another lender. And in case you are wondering why I used different interest rates, see Chapter 10.

CHAPTER SEVEN

THE 30-YEAR FIXED RATE MORTGAGE

With interest rates still historically low, the big question is whether a 30-year fixed rate mortgage is the right choice for your next home. While the mass media's response is usually yes, my reply is *no*. The media and big lenders advertise that you should "lock in" at a low rate and not worry about having your interest rate and payment adjust up at some future date. But is that good advice?

Today's real estate market is very different than both the market and lifestyle of the previous generation. This is why I do not advocate taking out a 30-year fixed rate mortgage.

As discussed in Chapter Three, prior generations had something called security. They typically had one job, a pension, one house and one mortgage. Today that lifestyle no longer holds true. Just look at the headlines in the business section each week and you will see that pension plans are becoming a thing of the past.

If you work for a public service agency or if you are a teacher you probably will be okay and your pension will be there when you need it. Or will it? Just do an Internet search on pension plans that have gone bankrupt or that are in jeopardy of going bankrupt. If you are employed in one of these industries you may want to put "plan B" into action just in case.

By now you are probably thinking, what does all of this have to do with a mortgage? Keep reading and you will see a method to my madness. Moving down the list comparing today's generation with the prior, you will find that most Americans will hold five or more jobs throughout their careers in several different industries. What number are you on? As far as houses and mortgages, the average family remains in a house for only seven years and according to Fannie Mae the average mortgage lasts roughly four years.

Why is this so? One of the reasons is that today we are a society of keeping up with the Joneses. Most Americans will own at least four houses. If you use real estate to create wealth by becoming a landlord or flipping properties you will own many more. But assuming you are the average American let's once again look at the homes you will own.

You buy your first house after renting for a while or when you become engaged and move out of your parents' house. This starter home will last you an average of three to seven years. Then you will want to move up the housing ladder. This starter home is the house that you stretched to afford to get out of the rental trap, to begin a family and to live the American Dream of owning your own home. But after a while you grow tired of this house and decide it is time for a new home, what I call the move-up home.

You may have built up some equity as discussed in the previous chapter, or perhaps you have two children, are in a two-bedroom home and you need more room. This move-up home will typically last five to 10 years depending upon where you live, the size of your family and of course how much you make. As you mature and make more money you want that house you have always dreamed about. You want the extra bedroom or that great room to entertain or perhaps you want more land for privacy. This third home is one that you will hold on to for 10 to 20 years while the kids go through high school and college. After this period maybe you will look to downsize because you are empty nesters and do not need that much room, or because you are near retirement and you want to move to another community. This last move will be in to typically the fourth and last home you will own.

But let's go back to your first or second home or even your dream house if you've found it and never plan on moving again. What type of mortgage should you take out?

Issues That Factor Into A 30-Year Mortgage:

- Is this a starter home or your long term home?
- Do you have student loans and other debt you need to pay off?
- Do you have (or plan to have) children?
    - If yes, consider whether you will have to pay for one of these in the future:
        - ✓ a Bat/Bar Mitzvah
        - ✓ a Quinceanera
        - ✓ a college education
        - ✓ a wedding
- Over the next 30 years do you think that you might lose your job and incur some debt as a result?
- Do you have elderly parents who might require long term health care?
- Do you want to put on an addition or upgrade your kitchen?
- Will your income change dramatically in the next three to five years?

If you answered yes to most or all of these questions, a 30-year fixed rate mortgage is probably *not* the right choice for you. All of the reasons listed above may trigger the need to refinance, and when that occurs the interest rate is not the driving force in the decision. Of course, you will want the best rate available at that time. But no matter what the rates are, you still need to refinance. My experience indicates that when people decide to refinance, only a small percentage of them refinance to lower interest rates. They refinance for the reasons suggested above or for strategic financial reasons as part of long term wealth building.

By now you are starting to realize that perhaps you don't want to take out such a long term mortgage but now you want to know what the choices and benefits are to the different types of mortgages. Chapter Three discussed the different types of mortgages available, so let's compare three of them.

Choosing an Adjustable Rate Mortgage (ARM), (see Chapter Eight for a full explanation) instead of a 30-year or even a 15-year fixed rate mortgage, can save you hundreds of dollars a month which will equate to thousands of dollars over just a few years. Also, keep in mind that 15 years into a 30-year fixed rate mortgage you still have *more than 71%* of the outstanding balance remaining. See graph.

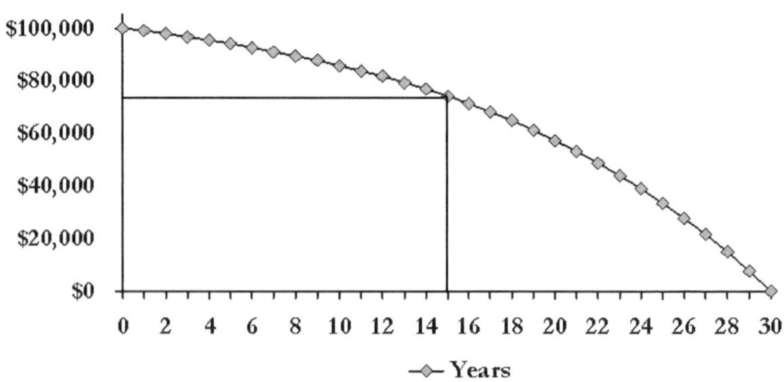

With the stage set, let's look at an example of an averaged-size mortgage. This illustration compares the payments for a $300,000 mortgage on a 30-year fixed rate schedule, a 5/1 ARM Interest Only mortgage (discussed in depth in Chapter Eight) and a progressive Cash Flow ARM mortgage (see Chapter Three for a refresher on this type of mortgage).

Three Common Mortgage Choices

	30-Year Fixed	5/1 ARM Interest Only	Cash Flow ARM minimum payment
Loan Amount	$300,000.00	$300,000.00	$300,000.00
Payment Rate	6.50%	6.00%	1.25%
Mo Payment	$1,896.20	$1,500.00	$964.92
Mo Savings		$396.20	$999.76
1st Yr Savings		$4,754.40	$10,757.39

As you can see, by choosing a mortgage other than a traditional 30-year fixed rate mortgage, you can free up money on a monthly basis. This will give you the ability to pay down those credit cards, re-direct the savings into a college fund or retirement fund, or create the ability to purchase a second home. Then there is the icing on the cake regarding tax planning.

When you have a typical amortizing mortgage (30-year fixed) you are paying both interest and principal payments each month. Each month you make your mortgage payment, the amount directed towards the interest decreases.

While this may sound like a good thing it actually may be bad. The analogy I like to use is: it is like driving through life with one foot on the gas and the other foot on the brake. You may still get where you want to go but it will take longer and your car will not be in great condition. Each year you earn more money (foot on the gas), while with every mortgage payment your tax deduction is getting reduced (the brake).

The chart below illustrates a 30-year fixed rate amortized loan in five year snap shots. You can see how the payment remains constant throughout the 30 years but notice how the "average interest" portion goes down significantly each year. The result is less tax savings each year.

30-YEAR FIXED RATE AMORTIZED MORTGAGE

YEAR		TODAY	5	10	15	20	25	30
MORTGAGE BALANCE	@ 6.500%	$300,000	$280,833	$254,328	$217,677	$166,996	$96,912	$0
PAYMENT	$1,896.20	$1,896	$1,896	$1,896	$1,896	$1,896	$1,896	$1,896
AVERAGE MONTHLY INTEREST		$1,625	$1,534	$1,395	$1,204	$939	$572	$65
MONTHLY TAX SAVINGS		$536	$506	$460	$397	$310	$189	$21
NET PAYMENT		$1,360	$1,390	$1,436	$1,499	$1,586	$1,707	$1,875

Chart provided by Forgotten Equity, Inc.

Your earnings are increasing and your deductions are decreasing because you are eliminating the income tax deductibility of mortgage interest with each payment. With an interest only mortgage, the mortgage interest deduction on your returns will remain constant for a certain number of years. This gives you the ability to keep more of your earnings and not pay them to the government.

"What is the interest rate" should be the *last question* you ask, not the first, when speaking with a mortgage planner. Unlike the lack of choices afforded to prior generations, there are literally hundreds of different mortgage products available. Hopefully by now you are realizing that choosing a mortgage today is much more complicated than "what is the interest rate".

CHAPTER EIGHT

ADJUSTABLE RATE MORTGAGES

This chapter breaks down the working components of **A**djustable **R**ate **M**ortgages (ARMs) so you know exactly how they work and therefore can be in a better position to determine if an ARM is right for you. They are really quite simple to understand once you know how the related components work.

Adjustable Rate Mortgages initially grew in popularity for first-time homebuyers during the mid-90s because they had lower interest rates than traditional 30-year fixed rate mortgages; lower interest rates correspond to a lower monthly payment. Over the years their use has grown tremendously and today they are commonplace for first time homebuyers as well as experienced investors. Since the turn of the new millennium, lenders have gotten very creative with the types of mortgages they offer and today you can get an ARM for as short as one month or as long as 10 years. The longer term ones are commonly referred to as "hybrid mortgages" by the media but they are ARMs nonetheless. They are called hybrids because they will have a fixed component for up to 10 years before they begin to adjust each and every year after the initial ten year period for the balance of the loan.

There are four different components that you need to be aware of for every type of ARM: the term, the index, the margin and the CAPs. As an example to refer to throughout this chapter we will use a **5/1 ARM** starting out at an interest rate of 6.25% based on the 12-Month Treasury Average Index, known as the "MTA Index," with a margin of 2.75% and CAPs of 5/2/5. I know that is a mouthful but once you understand each component you will know exactly what type of ARM you have or are being quoted and how it affects *you*. If you currently have an ARM program you can pull out the loan Note that you received at the closing. Paragraph four of that Note will explain how your mortgage will adjust.

Term: "5/1 ARM"

Let's break down the "5/1 Arm" one component at a time. *Term* refers to the first number — "5" — of the "5/1 ARM." This tells you the "type" of ARM that you will end up with. As mentioned above, the term of an ARM can vary anywhere from one month to 10 years. In this example, 5/1 Arm, the term of the ARM is five years.

No matter what term you choose the *total length of the mortgage* is usually 30 years. Popular ARMs are quoted as a 1 year ARM, 3/1 ARM, 5/1 ARM, 7/1 ARM or a 10/1 ARM and you need to know what the numbers mean. Less commonplace, you can also get a six month or even monthly ARM and they will work much the same as the others.

The first number in this type of ARM refers to a fixed period of time during which your interest rate and monthly payment will *not* change. The second number refers to how often the interest rate will adjust after the initial fixed period expires. As indicated above, these types of mortgages are sometimes referred to as "hybrids" because they have a fixed component (the first number) for a certain number of years and an adjustable component (the second number) for the remaining length of the mortgage.

In our example, a 5/1 ARM is a mortgage that will have a fixed period for the first five years and then the interest rate will adjust once a year on the anniversary of the loan for the balance of the loan beginning on the 61st month (that is, five years out) *if* you remain in the program. So, if you have a 3/1 ARM or a 7/1 ARM it simply means your "fixed rate" period is for the first three years and the first seven years, respectively. Some ARMS will have a "6" as the second number in the series. That means that the interest rate will adjust every six months after the initial period, not every year. It does ***not*** mean that the interest rate adjusts every six years.

INDEX

The index part of the mortgage refers to the business world benchmark to which the interest rate is tied or linked. Lenders will offer different programs based on the index or indexes of their choice. Some of the more common ones are: The 11th District Cost of Funds (COFI), the Monthly Treasury Average (MTA), The One Year Treasury Bill and the London Interbank Offer Rate (LIBOR). And no, that last one is not the bank of London. Rather it is a weighted opinion of a dozen or so international banks used for overnight lending. This index typically moves in pace with the Federal Funds Rate that we have all come to know through the Fed meetings now chaired by Ben Bernake and previously by Alan Greenspan.

Although your lender should explain this up front, the actual documents you will sign at a closing will indicate the index your mortgage is tied to, where you can find it and how the rate is applied to you. Usually you will not have a choice as to which index to choose as different lenders prefer one index over the other. Some will rise and fall faster then others because they are a leading market index which means that they go up and down with the current headlines. It's kind of like the instant news we can watch on cable TV. Others will be a moving or weighted average over 12 months and therefore they will be slower to change. Typically if we are in a rising interest rate environment, the weighted average indexes will rise more slowly. However, if we move to a declining environment they will stay higher longer. A great example is to look back at the period between January 2004 and January 2006 when interest rates were on a steady rise for two years. During this period the moving average indexes like the MTA were much lower than the others. Then during the second half of 2006 into 2007, since the interest rates essentially stabilized—as all the indexes were roughly within a quarter of a point of each other—until the downward trend in the fall of 2007 began.

A way to visualize this is by thinking of a rollercoaster with 12 cars on it representing 12 months. The lead car will always be the one to experience the immediate environment while the last car is way behind the times. As you climb the hill of the rollercoaster the front car will be the highest and as it starts the downward slide it will be the lowest. This is what it is like to be a leading index. The MTA or other average indexes are roughly the mid-point of the chain of cars. If the rollercoaster is on a flat section of track (much like the period between July 2006 and September 2007) the experience (interest rates) will be much the same.

Margin

This is a key component because this figure is added to your index and it will ultimately determine your actual interest rate as your loan comes into its adjustment periods (*limited by the CAPs, which are discussed below*). For most ARMs, the margin is set by the actual provider of the loan, and the consumer has little or no control. However, a larger margin on the Option ARM programs (discussed in Chapter Three typically) equates to more money for your lender, so feel confident and comfortable in asking your lenders to disclose the amount of money they are making on your loan and what would happen to their commission if they reduced the margin. Every lender has a right to make a good living, but not at your expense. They should fully disclose this to you and offer you the opportunity to pay this fee by way of points (discussed in Chapter Eleven) rather than have it be a part of your interest rate. Again it may not matter if you don't plan on staying in the ARM program after the initial fixed period but you should know the consequences anyway.

CAPs: "5/2/5"

CAPs refer to the limits on how your mortgage can adjust. This component of the mortgage will always come in a series of three numbers and we are using **5/2/5** in our example. This part of the mortgage can be the most complicated and is often the portion that is left out of a proposal by a lender to the consumer. It will be in the fine print and required disclosures but most loan officers will gloss over it.

- The **first number** in the series refers to the maximum amount your interest rate can go *up* or *down* on the **first adjustment date**. In this example it is **5** percentage points.
- The **second number** in the series refers to the maximum amount your interest rate can go *up* or *down* for **each and every change thereafter**. In this example it is **2** percentage points.
- The **third number** in the series refers to the **lifetime cap** that your interest rate can reach. In this example it is **5** percentage points.

Now that we know what all of the components are for an ARM, lets see how this applies to our example of a 5/1 ARM starting out at 6.25% with a margin of 2.75% and CAPs of 5/2/5.

As you near the end of the fifth year in our example you will receive a notice from your lender that your interest will be adjusting and they will tell you what the new rate will be. This is not an arbitrary increase as it is based upon the published index (usually in the *Wall Street Journal*) for your program. To this published rate they will add your MARGIN, as limited by your first adjustment CAP, and that will be your rate for the next 12 months. The formula is:

Your Index + Margin (*limited by your first CAP*) = New Rate

So let's go back and look at how our hypothetical mortgage might adjust. Since we started out at an initial rate of 6.25% the loan can increase by a CAP of five percentage points on the first change for a maximum interest rate of 11.25%. Let's say that at the first change date the index for our program was 9.00%. We would then add our Margin of 2.75% and come up with a proposed rate of 11.75%. But since we are limited by our first CAP of a maximum of five, our new interest rate for the sixth year (the 61st month through the 72nd) would be 11.25%. If the index was 7.00%, we would add our margin of 2.75% and come up with a new rate of 9.75% which is within the five-point CAP for our first change.

The Second Anniversary Date

This formula will be used to determine each and every other change for our mortgage on its anniversary date. However, after the first adjustment date, the CAP is controlled by the second number in the series of CAPs. In our example the second number is a "2." This means that after the first adjustment, each year's subsequent adjustment, up or down, cannot exceed two percentage points. Let's say that at the first change date the index for our program is at 5.00%. We would then add our Margin of 2.75% and come up with a new rate of 7.75% for the sixth year (the 61st month through the 72nd month). At the next anniversary going into the seventh year, the index is now at 8.00% to which we add our margin of 2.75% and come up with a proposed rate of 10.75%. However, since our CAP is set at 2% over the existing rate, the new rate applied to our mortgage would be limited to 9.75% for the seventh year, or months 73 through 84. This formula will be applied each and every year for the remaining life of the loan if you remain in the mortgage for the full 30 years.

But remember we still have a third number in the series of CAPs. This number means that no matter what happens, the maximum interest rate we could ever have is "capped." In our example that number is a "5," so no matter what happens our loan is capped at five percentage points over where we began. The interest rate on our example can *never* be more than 11.25%. So if you end up keeping your ARM beyond the first change date, your interest rate will adjust each and every year (or six months, if you have that program) within a set range, so if rates ever get really high again you will be protected.

Now that you know how an ARM works, let's look at what you might be facing with your mortgage if you closed five years ago and you took out a 5/1 ARM. Remember, this means that your interest rate and mortgage payment cannot change for the first 60 months of your loan. Depending upon the program you have, the first change to your interest rate may increase from a minimum of two to a maximum of six percentage points above your initial rate. Let's further assume the index that controls how your rate is determined is the LIBOR and the margin indicated in paragraph four of your Note is 2.75%. At the time of writing, the LIBOR index was 5.32%. The chart below illustrates how a mortgage would adjust in the beginning of the sixth year depending upon the CAP your program has.

Original Loan $420,000

	Traditional	Interest Only
Initial Rate	4.75%	5.00%
Initial Payment	$2,190.32	$1,750.00
Loan balance beginning of 6th year assuming all regular payments were made	$401,411.00	$420,000.00

6% CAP Illustration

New Rate	10.75%	11.00%
New Payment	$3,861.95	$3,850.00
Payment Increase	$1,671.63	$2,100
Percent Increase	76.32%	120.00%

2% CAP Illustration

New Rate	6.75%	7.00%
New Payment	$2,773.39	$2,450.00
Payment Increase	$583.07	$700.00
Percent Increase	26.62%	40.00%

In this example, the rates adjust upward significantly, as do the payments. If such increases were not a known or planned event, you could find yourself in trouble.

Chapter Nine

Interest Only Mortgages

Over the last decade and especially since the beginning of the new millennium, interest only mortgage mortgages have become very popular. I use them with the majority of our clients as part of a comprehensive mortgage plan, but many people are simply using them to be able to afford a house for which they otherwise could not qualify. Many of these mortgages are a subset of Adjustable Rate Mortgages (ARMs) and they have the same components (review Chapter Eight). Others have a fixed component that applies after the interest only period. Just as with regular ARMs, you can get an interest only mortgage for as short as one month or as long as fifteen years.

The big difference with these mortgages is that you are only paying interest on the borrowed funds; your original loan amount will **not** decrease with each payment! However, if you stay with the loan, this period will end (*in five, 10 or 15 years depending on the program*). Eventually you will be required to pay back both interest **and** principal just like a regular adjustable rate mortgage or on a 20-year fixed rate amortization schedule if you have that program. Now, this may sound like you will never get ahead or pay down your mortgage, but when used correctly these mortgages can be very effective.

You can create a heightened tax deduction and build vast wealth by using Interest Only mortgages the right way. Most pundits and the general media state that people who take out these mortgages will be in a world of trouble when the interest only time period wears off or when the interest rate adjusts upward. But they fail to look at the benefits that can result from the proper use of these mortgages. If you are using interest only mortgages simply to afford a house you couldn't otherwise buy, then yes, you may be exposed to difficult times ahead. However, if you use these as part of a comprehensive mortgage plan, you can invest the difference between the payments from these mortgages versus those of a 30-year fixed rate or another amortized type of mortgage and increase your wealth. This is the *key strategy* to using interest only mortgages.

I teach the majority of our clients to invest the monthly savings from these mortgages in an account with a financial planner. Even using a conservative return for the account, your money will perform better than by paying down the mortgage balance. Over time you will actually build up enough money in this account to pay off your loan quicker than by using a typical 30-year fixed rate mortgage.

Let's compare investing the difference in monthly payments of a $300,000 30-year fixed at 6.625% vs. a 5/1 interest only ARM at 6.25%. The difference in rates is due to the difference in programs, as an adjustable rate mortgage typically has a lower interest rate than a 30-year fixed rate mortgage. The 30-year fixed monthly payment would be $1,920.93 and the 5/1 interest only ARM payment would be $1,562.50 for a monthly savings of $358.43 that you will invest. The comparison would yield the following results:

Savings invested in an account earning a 6.50% rate of return			
Monthly Savings	**Annual Savings**	**Year**	**Year End Balance Compounded**
$358.43	$4,301.16	1	$4,453.59
$358.43	$4,301.16	2	$9,207.50
$358.43	$4,301.16	3	$14,279.78
$358.43	$4,301.16	4	$19,691.77
$358.43	$4,301.16	5	$25,472.94

In this example if you continued along with the program and you did not touch the investment account you would have sufficient funds in this account to pay your loan in full by the 23rd year. This approach will accomplish paying off your loan in roughly the same timeline as a bi-monthly program but without making the "extra" payments and without any more out of pocket expenses. You will also have a heightened income tax deduction, thus creating more take-home pay because you are not paying down the balance and reducing your interest expense. We actually advise our clients to meet with their CPA to plan their deductions so they will have more money each month in their paycheck rather than claim a big refund at tax time. In addition, by keeping your funds separated you have more liquidity than if the equity were tied up in your home. This allows you access to *your* money in the event of an opportunity or catastrophe.

Paying It Down

But, what if you are a believer in paying down your mortgage as fast as you can to get rid of the evil expense of a mortgage? Well you can still pay it off quicker than a traditional 30-year fixed but not as quickly as in the illustration above. So let's look at what would happen to your loan balance if you decided not to put the savings into a savings account but rather chose to send them in to your lender as "principal payments," lowering your balance at the end of every year. Assume the same factors as above.

Five Year Summary of Interest Only Compared to 30-Year Fixed				
30-year	Year End Balance	Year	Interest Only	Year End Balance
$1,920.93	$296,725.60	1	$1,562.50	$295,700.00
$1,920.93	$293,227.56	2	$1,540.10	$291,130.00
$1,920.93	$289,490.61	3	$1,516.30	$286,330.00
$1,920.93	$285,498.43	4	$1,491.30	$281,230.00
$1,920.93	$281,233.58	5	$1,464.74	$275,830.00

As you can see, simply by applying the monthly savings to your mortgage balance, you will be able to pay off the loan more quickly than by traditional methods. When you have an interest only mortgage, each time you send in a "principal payment" your next payment will be *lower* than the previous one since the payment is calculated on your current balance. This means that the difference in monthly payments between both types of mortgages will get larger each month. Here you will not be able to pay it off as quickly as in the earlier illustration because you are not earning the compound interest on the growing investment.

Send in a principal payment, and the next month, your monthly payment will **decrease**! If you're the type that likes to send in extra payments once a year or with each payment, these results get turbo charged. Under a 30-year fixed rate mortgage, sending in extra payments will not reduce your next month's payment; it stays the same. With interest only mortgages, you send in an extra principal payment and the next month your monthly payment decreases. Say you receive a bonus at work or you sell another asset and you want to apply $20,000 towards your balance at the end of the third year. Under the illustration above, your mortgage balance would then be reduced to $266,330. With an interest only mortgage your next month's payment would now be only $1,387.14, creating a savings of $533.79 compared to the 30-year payment. Add this amount to your investment account or increase how much principal you send to the lender and you can really build that investment account balance or further reduce your mortgage balance. I think you can see the snowball affect this would have.

Again if you are of the mindset of getting rid of your mortgage as fast as you can, an interest only mortgage may prove to be the better choice. An interest only loan will enable you to do this much more quickly than a typical loan with both interest and principal components would.

When Interest Rates Rise

I know you are saying: Yes, but what happens if rates increase? Even if your mortgage interest rate increases, you will still be able to pay off your loan faster with an interest only mortgage than you can with a standard mortgage because you will have a lower balance if you were paying it down. If rates do adjust upward to 7.00% in the sixth year, your interest only payment would increase *slightly* to $1,609.01 from the $1,562.50 payment you were making. The new payment was calculated from the reduced balance of $275,830.00, as shown in the chart on the opposite page. The monthly savings versus the 30-year mortgage would still be $311.92 and the cycle would still work. Also, if the cost of borrowing increases, so will the rate of return on your investment since rates are relative. If rates come down again, this strategy really takes off, as the monthly savings on the difference in payments will be greater.

No matter what your opinion (as to paying down your mortgage or not), when used correctly interest only mortgages may be the best choice because they give you greater flexibility. They allow you access to capital while also enabling you to create greater wealth.

Chapter Ten

Interest Rates

As a mortgage planner who works with clients from all walks of life, I am often asked "*how come my friend got a lower rate*?" In fact, when a repeat client of mine asked me this question in February 2006, it prompted me to write an article explaining much of the content that inspired this book. I always try and explain why variations in interest rates happen to individuals. The usual answer is that people are comparing apples to oranges. In that particular circumstance my client was mistaken about the type of mortgage her friend had. Upon questioning, she understood the difference. My client (who had just purchased her new home) was recently separated, had no job, never worked and could not prove her alimony as it was not yet part of a property settlement agreement. We were able to obtain a loan to buy her house using what is known as a "no documentation jumbo program". By contrast, her friend was gainfully employed, was able to verify her earnings as well as her assets and applied, as most people do, using a full documentation program.

In the above example the differences were easily distinguished. Many people, however, are under the impression that if the fellow down the street has a new 30-year fixed rate mortgage, then *they* should have the same rate. The problem with this assumption is that there are multiple factors that are missing from the equation. You and your friend might have the same "type" of mortgage, be it a 30-year fixed, 5/1 ARM or some other type, but *how* your rate is determined is much more complex than the type of mortgage you have.

Some factors that distinguish one mortgage from another that help determine a person's interest rate are, among others:

- ✓ credit score
- ✓ documentation type
- ✓ size of the loan
- ✓ loan-to-value ratio
- ✓ lock-in date
- ✓ type and location of property

In addition, different rates may apply from one person to another, depending upon whether it is a cash-out, or rate-and-term refinance, or a purchase. As you can see, even if it is the same type of loan and the rate was locked at about the same time, rates may still be drastically different due to many other factors. Let's break down each factor so you have a better understanding of what affects your interest rate.

The first factor to consider is when you locked in your interest rate. Unlike years ago, today's interest rates on mortgages can change weekly and even daily. By just looking at the fluctuations on an interest rate chart you see what I mean. The next determining factor directly relates to your credit scores. The higher your score, the lower the rate you will be offered. As we reviewed in Chapter One, the magic number you want to stay above is 720. Anything below this could have a negative effect on your interest rate.

The location of your property may play a minor role in determining your rate. For instance, mortgage rates in Manhattan are generally ⅛ to ¼ percentage point higher than those for the same type of mortgage in New Jersey. In addition, the type of property you are mortgaging will affect your rate. The best rates are reserved for owner occupied, full documentation, single-family residences. From this starting point your interest rate may increase if it is a multiple family dwelling, investment property, vacation home or one located in a high-rise condo complex.

Next on the list of things that may affect your interest rate is the size of the loan. Is it a conforming or jumbo loan amount? For 2007 the threshold for going into the jumbo market from the conforming market is a loan above $417,000. This figure usually goes up slightly each year and it is announced in the December time frame for the following year. Anything above this amount up to $750,000 falls into jumbo pricing and may have a higher rate. Loan amounts above $750,000 are classified as super jumbo by most lenders and rates may be even higher.

Another factor on the list is referred to as LTV. This acronym references the Loan-To-Value ratio of a mortgage. A 75 LTV would exist for a $300,000 mortgage for a property that is valued at $400,000. You can figure out your LTV simply by dividing your loan amount by the value of your property. Once you get over an 80 LTV your interest rate may again increase. If you have two loans, it is referred to as a CLTV or Combined Loan-To-Value. If you are buying or refinancing a home with 10% down, with one mortgage at 80% and a second mortgage at 10% you would have a CLTV of 90% and your rate may be higher than that of a person with only one mortgage at 80%. Refer back to Chapter Six for a review of this type of transaction.

The last and sometimes biggest factor to consider is the type of documentation required for you to get your mortgage approved. Sometimes you are required to supply what seems like your firstborn child and other times you don't have to supply anything. The type of loan documentation helps mortgage lenders decide on the type of mortgage and/or the amount for which a specific borrower can get approved. This is where the experience of your mortgage planner really comes into play. Your mortgage planner should be able to recommend the most suitable loan documentation type that fits your circumstances and financial needs, while being mindful of the headache for you in finding the correct documents to provide to the lender. In many cases, each time you provide less information to the lender the interest rate may increase and/or the LTV may decrease.

The reason for this increase is that the lender is providing you with money without all of the information as to its risk level regarding you. The higher the lender perceives its risk to be, the higher the interest rate it will charge. In addition, as you provide less information to the lender, it may limit how much it is willing to lend. Sometimes there is a direct correlation between the size of the loan, the LTV and documentation type. As documents are reduced, the size of the loan and the LTV will often be lowered.

Lenders have their own sets of guidelines and your mortgage planner will know which ones to seek out to shop for your mortgage approval. While there are sub categories of each documentation level depending upon the ultimate lender, below is an overview of the most common. Most of the different levels will require a two-year continuous employment history in the same industry unless stated otherwise.

Full Documentation

This is just what it sounds like and it is the most common type of loan program given. The lender will want to see everything about you. While these loans may have the lowest interest rates compared to other documentation types they may not always be the best alternative. Not only will the lender verify your employment, your income (30 days' worth of pay stubs) and all of your assets (two months' worth of statements) they may also want to see your income tax returns (personal and business if self-employed) and W-2s for the past two years. This can be a burden as the lender will want to see all the pages of each document. Many clients choose to go with a less intrusive documentation type for various reasons: they don't want to be bothered with finding all of the correct documentation; they are self-employed or their tax returns are complicated; their tax returns were not completed; or their mortgage planner determined that he could get them the same rate as a full document loan, but with a lesser documented type and less of a burden to the client.

STATED INCOME – VERIFIED ASSETS (SIVA)

Under these types of programs, you can "state" what your income is on the application but the lender will not actually verify what you make. Some lenders will require that you certify on IRS Form 4506 that the amount you state is what you report on your tax returns; other lenders do not require this step. These types of loans work well for clients who are self-employed and/or are commissioned sales people with sporadic earnings. While the borrower does not have to provide tax returns and pay stubs, the lender will verify the place of employment as well as require copies of all the statements for the assets disclosed on the application, just as they do under a full documentation loan.

STATED INCOME – STATED ASSETS (SISA)

Under these types of programs, you "state" what your income is on the application and you "state" what your assets are. Here the lender will not verify the income or assets that you state. They may, as with SIVA loans discussed above, require that you certify on IRS Form 4506 that the amount you state as your income is what you report on your tax returns. Disclosure of employment is required. Your place of employment will be verified by the lender and that you have worked there for as long as you stated on the application. No asset documentation is required or verified.

No Ratio

Under this program income is not disclosed, stated or verified but your assets are disclosed and stated. The lender will verify the place of employment as well as require copies of all statements for the assets disclosed on the application for verification, as they do under a full documentation loan.

No Income And No Asset (NINA)

The income and assets are not disclosed, stated or verified on the application. Disclosure of employment is required and it will be verified by the lender that you work there and have for as long as you stated on the application. Income will not be discussed or verified during this process.

No Documentation

This is just what it sounds like. In essence, the lender will provide you with a mortgage based upon the fact that you ask for it and you have a good credit score. You do not have to have a job. This is often used when a client is not working or if they do not have a two-year continuous employment history. Many times this will be used if you recently went back to work after staying at home for a while or if you were laid off and just went back to work. The interest rate will be higher than that for the other types of documented loans discussed above but at least you can get the loan you need. As this book was going to press this type of mortgage went away. I chose to leave the information here in case they come back. Also, many of the loans that are going into foreclosure were of this type; it is no wonder that many people used this type of program for houses they could not afford.

As you can see, the rate you are quoted is much more complex than what you may read in the paper that day or see online at various mortgage sites. Your rate is a delicate balance of LTV, credit score, and documentation type as well as the other factors outlined above. Your mortgage planner should be well versed in all of the above. His or her expertise in the documentation type as well as type of mortgage program to recommend should go hand in hand.

Typically you would not put a no-documentation client into a 30-year fixed rate mortgage. This is because any good planner will understand that the client's circumstances may change in the next year or two. By starting off in an ARM program you will have a lower interest rate than in a 30-year fixed mortgage. Then, once your circumstances change for the better, you can improve upon your program. This approach will make the best use of your cash flow and provide you with the best situation to keep more money for investments. Once the conditions change, you will be able to fully document your situation. At that time, you can refinance into a better program and reduce your interest rate significantly. For further discussion on the type of mortgage that is right for you, review Chapter Seven.

CHAPTER ELEVEN

MORTGAGE POINTS

You've seen the ads and heard them on the radio: No cost loans! or No points! Perhaps you've seen a rate quoted in the newspaper that seems too good to be true. Then, when you call or read the fine print, you find out that you must pay a "point" or two in order to get that rate. The problem is that no one really explains what a point is, or if they do, they usually don't advise you on whether you should consider paying these points. This chapter will explain what a point is and then lay out a formula that you can use to determine if it makes sense for you to pay one with your next mortgage. So let's start with the basics.

A point or a fraction thereof is simply a fee that you pay in order to get your interest rate discounted below what the rate would be if there were no points paid. Simply put, a point is one percent (1.00%) of the loan amount for which you are applying. Two points would be two percent (2.00%) of the loan amount.

Let's say you are applying for a $300,000 mortgage and you are quoted a rate of 6.25%, with one point in order to get that rate. This means that you will have a fee due at the closing in the amount of $3,000 ($300,000 x 0.01) payable to the lender or broker. If you are quoted a rate with ½ point or ⅜ of a point it is again simply a fraction of your loan amount. For a $300,000 mortgage these would be $1,500 (for ½ pt) or $1,125 (for ⅜ pt). If you are not sure how to calculate three eighths of a point, it is easy. Every ⅛ is one eighth of one percent (1.00 ÷ 8 = 0.125) so you would just multiply 0.125 times 3 to get the answer of 0.375%. The formula for determining the fees above would be $300,000 x 0.005 = $1,500.00 or $300,000 x 0.00375 = $1,125.00.

Now that you know what a point is and how it is calculated, you need to understand how to determine if it makes sense for you to pay a point or fraction of one for your loan. There used to be an old rule of thumb that if you planned on living in your home for more than five years then it made sense to pay points. Today however that rule does not really apply. The real question is "how long do you plan on having this mortgage?" Due to life-changing events (job, college, renovations, etc.), a mortgage does not really last as long as you stay in a home. As we learned earlier, the average mortgage lasts roughly 4.2 years. So, should you pay points on your next loan?

Assuming that you have the additional funds to pay for the points at the closing, let's determine if it makes sense for you to do so. We will be using an example of a $300,000 mortgage for a 5/1 ARM that is amortized, as well as an interest only example. The choices you may be presented with might be:

<u>An Amortized loan consisting of both principal and interest</u>

6.375% interest rate with zero points = monthly payment of $1,871.61

-vs-

6.125% interest rate with a ½ point = monthly payment of 1,822.83

Although the rate is one quarter percent lower, it does not have the effect on the monthly payment that you might think. The monthly savings is only $48.78, or $585.36 a year. The focus should be on the monthly payment and not the rate: the name of the game is cash flow. If you choose the discounted rate, it will come with the expense of $1,500.00 due at the closing.

You now have to figure out how long it will take before you make back the $1,500.00 cost you expended to get the lower rate. After you make up the cost, any savings are gravy.

The formula for this is very simple. You take the total cost of the points and divide that by the monthly savings of the lower rate. In this example the formula is $1,500 ÷ $48.78 = 30.75. What this means is that it would take you just under 31 months to make back the cost you incurred to get the lower rate and payment. After that you would be ahead of the game with the monthly savings. So, if you plan on having this mortgage for three years or longer it looks like it makes sense to pay the ½ point up front to get the lower rate. If you do not keep the mortgage for at least three years it would be a waste of money. This basic formula can be used no matter how many points you choose to pay to get a lower rate. The formula is:

Cost of point(s) ÷ monthly savings = number of months to recoup cost

In addition, with the amortized loan used in the above example, you would also be $429.79 ahead of the game as far as your loan balance is concerned. At the higher rate you would have a balance of $290,663.36 after 31 months, whereas with the lower rate your balance would be $290,233.57. Although under this illustration there is not much of a difference, it is still a number of which you should be aware.

If you were applying for an interest only mortgage, the calculation would be the same. Again, assuming a $300,000 mortgage for a 5/1 Interest Only ARM, the choices you may be presented with might be:

6.5% interest rate with zero points = monthly payment of $1,625.00

-vs-

6.25% interest rate with a ½ point = monthly payment of $1,562.50

Under this illustration your monthly savings would be $62.50 with the discounted rate. Once again, you would have $1,500.00 due at the closing. The formula to determine if this makes sense for you is exactly the same as above: $1,500 ÷ $62.50 = 24. As you can see, under the interest only example it only takes 24 months to make back the cost you incurred to get the lower rate.

The savings in both examples is what we refer to as the gross savings, without considering other factors that should go into the formula. One factor to consider is the tax deductibility of the point. You should seek the advice of a CPA to determine the effect for you. There are different rules that apply depending on whether we are discussing a primary residence versus an investment property and a purchase versus a refinance. Generally speaking you can deduct the point(s) from your taxes in the year they were paid if they are for a mortgage on your primary residence and they were not used to cover items that are normally charged on the HUD-1 Settlement Statement such as title fees, appraisals, etcetera. Any points that do not meet these requirements generally can be deducted over the life of the loan.

There are several other factors that go into the deductibility determination. To see if the points you paid or are thinking of paying are deductible, I advise you to seek the advice of a CPA. You can also learn more about this subject by reading IRS Publication 936 www.irs.gov/publications/p936/index.html and IRS Topic 504 - Home Mortgage Points by visiting the IRS website at www.irs.gov/taxtopics/tc504.html.

Another factor to consider is the "opportunity cost." By using the $1,500 to pay the point, you do not have that money available for other investments. If you were able to earn 6.00% on this money, it might grow to $1,786.52 after three years. Having this money to invest may or may not be a good thing depending upon your savings and investing history. If you, like most people, are not good at saving then it may make sense for you to pay the point.

CHAPTER TWELVE

DEBT CONSOLIDATION

Now, I know that mainstream financial writers and planners will disagree with my advice in this chapter. But by now you can see that I am not a mainstream thinker. My goal in the advice we give our clients and people who read what I write is: How can I improve their financial well-being? With that said, would you pay an interest rate of 16% or more for your mortgage? *(Putting the late '70s and early '80s aside.)* Of course not! But if you carry credit card debt you are probably paying at least this much, and these payments are not tax deductible.

I know that we incur credit card debt because sometimes we are dealt a bad hand in life. All of a sudden you need a new furnace or some other unplanned catastrophe occurs. Sometimes it is because you can't control your urges, wants and desires. Sometimes it is because you just lost your job, you had a serious illness or for a host of other reasons. But many times it is as a result of a vicious cycle that occurs every year — holiday spending. No matter what the reason, if you regularly carry credit card debt you can take the lesson from this scenario and apply it across the board.

Every year we incur more and more credit card debt. As mentioned above, one of the largest culprits is the holiday season. During this time we spend record amounts on gifts that friends and relatives really did not need with money that we really didn't have. Worse, beginning in January you receive the first of several credit card statements and you quickly realize that you spent more than you had planned and you can't pay it off in one payment. So your plan is to systematically pay off all of the holiday gifts by summer. Many Americans have those good intentions and that is one reason bankruptcies and foreclosures are reaching new highs.

Even if you follow your plan and are able to make the minimum payments, you will never be able to get ahead. Over time you will end up paying two to five times the cost of the item instead of simply paying in cash originally or paying the credit card in full when you received your first statement. But since the average person is living paycheck to paycheck, sometimes that isn't a possibility. People are finding that suddenly they need new tires, brakes, the refrigerator is on the fritz, the hot water heater blows or one of the children needs braces. The result is a few missed credit card statements or worse—a missed mortgage payment. Your credit score goes down and the interest rate on your credit cards go up. This in turn increases your minimum payment. It's not hard to see how many people can get into trouble very quickly.

Carrying Debt Prevents You From Saving

Each month you have three major spending categories: your mortgage, your credit card bills and your retirement accounts. When you're short on money, one will get squeezed out. Can you guess which one it is? Many books and articles have been written that detail this phenomenon: if you carry debts other than your mortgage you will never be able to get ahead and carrying debt prevents you from saving. You will struggle all year to get your credit cards paid off and then the holidays hit again and the cycle starts all over.

As homeowners, you may have another choice. It *may* make sense for you to tap the equity that has built up over the years and consolidate your debts into one payment. This approach will often reduce your monthly obligations and possibly increase your tax deductions. A strategic refinance to consolidate your debts can also free up cash you can actually invest towards your retirement. Now, you might be thinking you are simply borrowing from Peter to pay Paul and that you are actually extending the overall cost of the credit card debt. But are you really? Here is an example of two of my clients in their 50s (we'll call them Mary and John) whom we helped out of this exact situation.

Mary and John had run up some significant debt on several credit cards and were referred to us by their accountant. Like many of us, life had gotten in the way and over the years they had amassed $35,000 in credit card debt in addition to three mortgages. They had no retirement savings. With an average interest rate of 23%, you can imagine that the minimum payments were killing them. We were able to structure a program for Mary and John that *reduced their overall monthly payments by $1,260—that is more than $15,000 per year*—and they now have positive cash flow every month.

We set them up with a financial planner who in turn instituted a methodical contribution plan setting aside half of this monthly savings for their retirement, while the other half goes into a fund to pay for sudden expenses. The fund will grow to a six-month cash reserve (enough to pay all their expenses should they lose their jobs). After the reserve fund has sufficient cash, the cash that had been going in there will be directed into their retirement savings. Mary and John are able to enjoy life again knowing they are not drowning in debt, they have money available for emergencies, and their retirement planning is now on track to attain their goals.

In the above situation we did increase the size of their mortgage and we also increased the time frame for them to pay it off. But they now have a mortgage plan that enables them to save for both short and long term goals. If they had not taken this approach, they would have continued to struggle and most likely never gotten out of debt. They would not have been able to create their retirement funds or meet their monthly obligations. As pointed out above, not being able to meet monthly payments causes good people to lose their homes.

CHAPTER THIRTEEN

ANNUAL PERCENTAGE RATE (APR)

The Annual Percentage Rate (APR) is one of the most confusing and misleading parts of the mortgage process. This is a figure that the federal government requires all lenders to disclose so you can compare loans offered by lenders. The APR is disclosed on the Federal Truth in Lending form (TIL). This document should always be presented with the Good Faith Estimate (GFE) of closing costs. The APR is meant to level the playing field and deter deceptive practices. The GFE shows the real cost of money. It is supposed to factor in the cost to the lender of borrowing the money for your loan, and it is a figure based upon the actual amount financed, and not the amount borrowed, which are usually different.

The problem is that APR is often meaningless unless you know how to calculate it. The information on one TIL and GFE may differ from another even though legally they are supposed to contain the same information. Therefore, it is a figure we advise our clients to ignore. I know that is not what we are told but unless you know exactly how it is calculated and what is listed on each TIL and GFE you will have a meaningless number.

Sadly most people in the industry do not even know how the APR is calculated. In fact, when I was a practicing real estate attorney and loan officers attended the closings, I would have some fun with them. When we came to the APR disclosure on the TIL form, I would look over to the loan officer and ask them to explain the document to the client. Very few actually knew how and would signal for me to explain it so they did not look bad in front of their clients. So of course I would simply continue and describe the document, which I will do momentarily.

But before I do I want to reiterate that we advise our clients to focus on the monthly payment when comparing loans. Again the advertised APR is meaningless *unless* you know *exactly* how it was calculated and *what* costs are built in to that rate. Yes we will compare the overall closing costs so see how long one loan will take to recoup the costs over another before we recommend one option over another and this is what the APR is supposed to do. But as stated above, the information used to calculate it is often not accurate. In addition, this is a number that can be manipulated up or down as the lender chooses and you really have no idea if it makes sense. In fact, many times a loan with a lower APR will not be the better choice.

The numbers you do have to compare are your monthly payments and your total closing costs charged by the lender, *excluding* the per diem (daily) interest charges. As indicated throughout this book the interest rate you are paying is not as important as how much you are paying each and every month. In addition, just as you need to see if it makes sense to pay points to lower your rate and payment (Chapter Eleven), you should perform a similar calculation when comparing one lender's closing costs with another's, remembering to exclude the per diem interest costs for your loan.

The reason for excluding per diem interest cost is that it is not a cost of the transaction in doing business with the lender. You are simply paying for the money (the daily interest charge) for the balance of the month in which you borrow the money.

> **Side note:** Mortgage payments are not like rent payments. Your June 1 rent payment applies to the month of June. You pay the amount *before* you use the month. However, mortgage payments work in just the opposite way. Your June 1 mortgage payment is for the month of May! You pay for the month *after* you use it. So if you close on June 5 you will have 26 days of per diem interest and your first mortgage payment will be due on August 1 for the month of July. If you close on June 25 your next payment will still be due on August 1, but you will have fewer days of per diem interest charged at your closing: six days to be exact.

You will pay a larger or smaller amount of per diem depending upon when you close your loan in any given month. Close at the end of the month and it will be lower than if you close at the beginning of the month. If you are buying your first house this could have a big impact on your overall closing costs. However, when refinancing or buying another home that involves selling your current home, it really does not matter. The reason it does not matter is that there will be per diem for your new loan as well as for the loan you are paying off. Close on the 20th of a month and you will have 11 days of interest on your new loan and 20 days interest on your old loan. Now that we have enough background on what APR is and is not, how do we actually calculate it?

How To Figure APR

In a nutshell, the APR is determined by taking the amount "financed" and dividing it by your mortgage payment.[7] The amount financed is always less than the actual amount borrowed because the lender is not going "out of pocket" for the full amount you are borrowing. Assuming you have a loan amount of $300,000 and bank fees including your per diem costs of $2,750, the bank would only be "financing" $297,250 because

[7] To obtain a sample copy and an explanation of a Truth In Lending disclosure visit www.mortgageswhatyouneedtoknow.com

you are paying "financing costs" in the amount of $2,750 the day of closing. Since you are paying the bank a certain amount to borrow their money, they are not really out of pocket for the entire amount you are borrowing. You are contributing or bringing to the closing, costs in the amount $2,750.00 that is payable to the lender. They only need to make up the difference of $297,250.00 to fund your loan amount of $300,000.00. Think of it this way, if you said to someone I'll give you two dollars now to let me borrow $10, they are only out of pocket $8. You still owe them $10 but the $2 was the cost of doing business. This is what is happening with the bank. You are still borrowing the $300,000 in this instance and that is the amount you owe, but the lender did not have to come up with all of it on the day of closing. Part of the money you borrow pays the lender's costs in procuring the loan money for you.

Some of the costs that get factored into the APR calculation are:

- ✓ Application fee
- ✓ Commitment fee
- ✓ Life of loan flood certification fee
- ✓ Funding fee
- ✓ Per diem interest charges
- ✓ Discount points
- ✓ Origination points
- ✓ Underwriting fees

These are only a sampling but you get the idea. The costs that go into calculating the APR are found in the "800 Section" of your GFE and eventual HUD-1 Closing Statement and are items paid to the lender. If they are listed here then they are generally included in the cost unless they were paid to any third party companies.

The following things, to name a few, are *not* included in the APR calculation, even if they are in the "800 Section":

- ✓ Your attorney's or closing agent's fees

- ✓ Title insurance
- ✓ Inspection fees
- ✓ Credit report fees
- ✓ Appraisal costs

HOW THE NUMBERS WORK

Even though I do not advocate 30-year fixed rate mortgages, since the interest rate is fixed for the entire period, I am going to use one to show you what I mean because in such an example, we know the cost of the money (your interest rate) over the entire life of the mortgage. When calculating the APR for an Adjustable Rate Mortgage we have to make assumptions (worst case scenario) of what will happen to the rate after the initial fixed period of the loan. This will make the APR even more meaningless than it already is as the interest rate chosen is just a complete guess.

Let's look at our example of a $300,000, 30-Year fixed rate loan:

Loan "A"	**Loan "B"**
Interest rate of 6.375%	Interest rate of 6.125%
Monthly payment $1,871.61	Monthly payment $1,822.83
Zero points	Zero points
Total Fees $967.00	Total Fees $3,967.00
APR of 6.42%	APR of 6.25%

Loan A has lower closing costs, a higher interest rate and a higher APR so, according to traditional thinking and what the government would have you believe, Loan B should be the better choice. With Loan B's lower interest rate and APR you will save $48.78 per month. But is it the better program? Loan B has $3,000.00 more in closing costs and it will take you 61 ½ months (five years) to make back that difference. In order to make the example "work" the way I wanted it to, I manipulated the numbers. In Loan A I have five days of per diem costs and I used 25 days' worth in Loan "B." I did this to prove that you should not be looking at the APR since you really do *not* know how it is calculated when you are mortgage shopping.

Again, the APR rate is not as important as the monthly payment unless you have *all* of the information, you can ensure the information is exactly the same on each TIL and you know how to calculate it. Make life less complicated; just look to what your proposed monthly payment will be, factor in the costs and run the calculations to determine which program is better for you.

CHAPTER FOURTEEN

THE HELOC LIFE JACKET

A home equity line of credit, also known as a HELOC, is a type of mortgage. Unfortunately, HELOCs often are not used appropriately or to their fullest advantage as financial planning tools. I recommend that all of our clients take out a HELOC right after we close on their new house (or refinance) because they make good life preservers in the event you need cash.

What if you suddenly become disabled or get laid off from your job? If you had taken out a HELOC while gainfully employed you would have the necessary funds to draw from to pay your bills. Once you are back on your feet you can simply pay off this loan and save it for another rainy day.

No one thinks this will happen to them. However, statistically you have a good chance of losing your job, while one of every three people reading this will become temporarily disabled during their lifetime. So if you don't like to leave things to chance, simply call your mortgage planner and ask him or her for a life preserver to keep your head above financial turmoil.

If you think that you will simply wait until you get laid off or become disabled and then apply for a HELOC, think again. You will be denied! *Banks only lend based upon your ability to demonstrate that you can make payments.* If you don't have a job or if you are not working you can't show the bank your ability to pay the money back; the bank will not extend the life jacket to you.

Think about it. If you are in a boat, normally you don't use the life jacket under your seat. But if the boat capsizes you will be very happy it was there. In the event life throws you a curve ball and you get thrown overboard, you will be glad you had taken out a HELOC while you were in good health and gainfully employed. While I do not advocate consuming your home's equity, a home equity line of credit can be like an insurance policy to ensure you do not lose your home during an economic downturn.

There is no cost (or at least there should not be) for this new line of credit unless you begin to write checks and draw against it. If you do use some of it you will only be charged for the money you use and not the entire amount for which you were approved. By being proactive in your finances and by making life happen you can have peace of mind; you will know that you have a source of money to pay bills should the unforeseen happen to you.

Furthermore, with an *unused* line of credit you are free to capitalize on opportunities should they arise. What if a great business comes along that you want to invest in, you see an investment property you want to purchase, or you decide that you want to or need to move? Having an *unused* HELOC at your disposal allows you to get in the game. For example, you will have the funds at your fingertips to make offers on a new house, using the equity from your existing house as a down payment. This is a trap that many people get into because they do not know the rules in the game of lending. They want to move but the money they need for a down payment is trapped in their homes.

THE BUY/SELL TRAP

Most people don't know this until it is too late. Here is how it typically plays out. You call a mortgage broker trying to get a mortgage for your new house and you need to close in 30 days. In addition, you just put your house on the market hoping it sells in time because you need the equity in your current home to use as a down payment on your new home. If it does not sell in time, you figure you will take out a HELOC to cover the required down payment and then sell your current house later. The problem with this is that *once your house is on the market banks will not lend you money on that house*! Unless you have a sale contingency in your contract to buy your new home you could have a big issue. If you had taken out a HELOC beforehand, as suggested in this chapter, you would be able to buy your new home under this scenario.

Be careful once you do get this new HELOC! All too often people act on all of the great advertising and marketing from corporate America coupled with the "I need that" mentality and get in trouble by spending HELOC funds on frivolous things such as vacations, boats, cars, Plasma TVs or any other consumer item. It is very tempting to use it for these things but money from a HELOC loan should only be used for the purpose for which you took it out: as a smart financial preservation tool. A life preserver!

Now you might be thinking: Hey, wait a minute. Didn't Chapter Twelve advise that home equity can be used to consolidate consumer debts? If you recall, in that chapter I did recommend this. But that was done as a financial strategy to right the ship — together with a mortgage plan to correct past bad behavior that is bringing a homeowner down, with the ultimate purpose of helping to get him afloat. Chapter Twelve showed how cash flow management strategies can be used to control spending and free up money to invest.

If you only learn one thing from this book let it be that you should call your mortgage planner **today** and ask him for a life preserver. Don't delay. You never know *when* life will happen to you.

CHAPTER FIFTEEN

AFTER THE CLOSING

You just purchased your home and closed on your new mortgage. You have reams of paperwork from your mortgage planner and attorney or closing agent. In addition, you don't even know what you just signed. You want to ensure that you have all of your information for a later date and you stuff all of it in a drawer somewhere. If you just refinanced your mortgage, it is likely that you will have more than one folder like this containing information from your past mortgages.

Here's a tip: You do not need all the paperwork.

After you close on your mortgage there are only three things you need to save;

1. Copy of the Mortgage
2. Copy of your Note
3. Copy of your HUD-1 or RESPA Settlement Statement

All other documents at this point are not necessary unless you are in a dispute with your lender. Then you need to retain everything. You should place the three documents referenced above in a file and put a cover sheet on top of them detailing what the terms of your mortgage are. Simply read paragraphs two, three and four of your Note, highlight the terms on the document, and write them down on your cover sheet and clip together. When we send out our confirmation of terms to our clients post-closing, we include copies of these three documents and provide them with a cover letter detailing their transaction. The middle portion of our client post-closing letter contains the following:

Furthermore, in case you forgot the terms and conditions of your loan we have detailed them below.

1st Loan Program:	10/1 ARM Interest Only
Interest Rate:	6.125%
Escrows:	Taxes only
Loan Amount:	$328,000
1st Rate Change:	August 1, 2017

I suggest that you model your cover sheet with this information. If we closed two mortgages for our client then we would have a few more rows detailing the second loan and its terms.

If you are in the mortgage business you may want to add this post closing touch to your practice. Your clients will certainly appreciate it.

Chapter Sixteen

Annual Review

Being proactive with your finances is how you make life happen. When it comes to your mortgage I suggest that you review your situation at least once a year. We do this with all of our clients and a good mortgage planner should be calling you on the anniversary of your closing for the same reason. Usually we mail out a letter and then follow up with a phone call just to confirm that our client is happy with his or her program and there have been no major life changes. If major changes have happened, we will have a lengthier conversation to see if we can help improve their finances.

We will review the value of their home to see if there has been any major change, as well as the terms of their mortgage, and whether they incurred some debts during the past year. A lot can happen in your life each year and you need to ensure that the program you and your mortgage planner selected at your closing still makes sense. Your home may have increased in value, your credit scores may have improved allowing for better mortgage rates, you may have taken out a home equity loan for improvements, or there could be a host of other needs such as college or retirement planning.

Lastly, as discussed in Chapter One, you should be reviewing your credit report each year to ensure that there are no unknown issues with it. By doing this on an annual basis you can help protect yourself against identity theft by identifying any unauthorized charges. Your mortgage planner should provide you with a credit report analysis once a year for free.

I suggest, since you have almost finished this book, that you begin your annual review right now! I know it is probably not the anniversary of your mortgage, but why not look today to see if you can improve your situation. See the Appendix for a Mortgage Check-Up form that you can use and even fax it in to your mortgage planner for a professional analysis. You can find additional forms by visiting www.mortgageswhatyouneedtoknow.com.

CHAPTER SEVENTEEN

CHOOSING A MORTGAGE PLANNER

A quality mortgage planner should be able to guide you through the maze of choices when it comes to buying your next home or refinancing your current mortgage. When I began writing this book there were more than 450,000 mortgage people in the country. I was putting the finishing touches on the book during the big mortgage meltdown of October 2007 and our industry was losing people by the tens of thousands.

Historically our industry has only had 250,000 or so "professionals" but the real estate boom between 2002 and 2006 brought many unqualified people into the field, lured by easy money. Many states don't even require an exam to become licensed to sell mortgages. For instance, in New Jersey a person can walk into a mortgage firm, ask for a job and minutes later be on the phone recommending a loan to a consumer. Hopefully the powers that be will institute national licensing requirements similar to licensed security brokers under the authority of the NASD. By doing this we can uphold a higher level of professionalism, have a body to file complaints with and finally have uniform disclosures across all states. But luckily, for now, it is becoming harder to earn a living in the mortgage industry and many unqualified loan originators are leaving to pursue the next big thing.

So how do you find and choose a quality mortgage planner?

One of the best ways is to ask your family and friends whom they used *and* whether they were happy with that person *and* would they use them again? Too many people today simply go to one of the major mortgage portals on the Internet and submit their information to get a "quote on a rate." The problem with this is the process allows for no planning and you don't know whom you are dealing with. In addition, by submitting your Social Security number to one of these web portals you will activate the "trigger lists" as discussed in Chapter Two—and you don't want that.

This may be your first mortgage or it may be your fifth. Either way, a good mortgage planner will be able to prescribe a better plan for you than you could on your own. After all, this is what they do for a living. Although this can occur over the phone during several lengthy conversations, I recommend that you choose one who is local to you so you can meet face-to-face at their office and ensure that they have your best interest at heart and that you get a good vibe. An added benefit is that a qualified planner is often a pillar of your community and as such may be able to refer you to other quality professionals to assist you in your life.

In addition, the quotes you receive from the online portals are often not accurate. This may be because they did not have a complete file. Quite often, all of the information you submitted online was not accurate. It wasn't that you willfully input wrong information. Rather, this occurred because you are not trained in this field and may be unfamiliar, for example, with terminology. A good mortgage planner would be able to extract the right information to research and prescribe the right program for you.

Even if you get referred to a mortgage planner by a friend, be sure to be proactive in the questions you ask him or her and don't simply let the person dictate what is best for you.

Remember, a mortgage is most likely the largest financial decision you will ever make. Perhaps you will make it several times throughout your life but don't make this type of decision in a couple of minutes over the phone, or worse, over the Internet late at night before you go to bed. Even if you are dealing with your local bank, you need to ensure the person you are dealing with is knowledgeable on all facets and not just there to take your order. Your financial well being depends on it.

Take the time to research all the products available and then sit down with a mortgage planner to discuss your options. Your goal in the meeting is to ensure he or she is knowledgeable on all programs and is interested in *you* as a client and not just there to take your order. When you find one you think is right for you, call them to schedule an appointment to meet in their office.

Don't give the excuse that you are "too busy" to meet them at their offices because that is a cop out. You go to your attorney's office for meeting. You go to your doctor's office for check-ups so why not your mortgage planner's? After all, the time spent here will most likely have a greater impact on your life overall. Also, by meeting them at their office you can gauge the type of business the planner has and if you want to work with this company. At this meeting feel free to ask them for resumes and/or credentials as to their experience. After all, they will be helping guide your financial future and you have a right to know their backgrounds.

Once you decide to go with a particular mortgage planner make sure he is able to provide you with a reason why you should or should not be in the program he is recommending to you. He should be able to offer you several options and a mortgage plan to accomplish your financial goals. Don't let him just push a mortgage on you.

Remember this should be a collaborative effort in choosing the right program for your needs. If he does not have the time to dedicate to you, thank him and look elsewhere. However, be mindful that his or her time is equally important and don't waste it. Think long term and be decent: If you have a good meeting and if you are satisfied with her expertise, engage her services for your mortgage. Don't take all of the time, expertise and information she has provided you and then go somewhere else because you can get the program you decided — with her help — was right for you, from another seller for a ⅛ or a ¼ of a point cheaper. That is not right and chances are if you switch to another person without researching him, you could be in for a bumpy ride. Over the years we have had several clients call us back after going with another lender only to find out that what the other lender said they could do ended up not panning out.

So as you are trying to find a quality planner to rely on, use these questions to see if they are qualified:

1. Is this your full-time or part-time job?
2. How long have you been in the mortgage business?
3. How do you get most of your clients?
4. Do you have any information I can read about your background and experience?

You should also Google the mortgage planner's name and company to see what you uncover. If good stuff comes up, then proceed. If bad information pops up, then I suggest that you look for another planner. If no information then you have a decision to make.

Now, when you ask the above questions, the planner doesn't have to come through with shinning results on every question. These questions are simply provided to give you a basis to form an opinion. People can be brand new to the industry but based on their former background can be very knowledgeable. Likewise, some can have 15 years in the business and only be an order taker and offer no planning advice.

After you have chosen the mortgage planner that you want to work with, what comes next? Here is a list of questions to ask when your mortgage planner presents you with a plan:

1. What will my monthly payment be, excluding escrows?

2. Is it an interest only mortgage, and if yes, for how long?

3. If it is an adjustable rate mortgage (ARM), ask him to explain and show you what the CAPs and margin are as well as the index to which it is tied. *(This will be detailed in the ARM disclosure that they are required to give you by law and that you will sign).*

4. Have your planner confirm the type of mortgage it is and ask her to put it in writing if you can't clearly determine this yourself.

5. If you think you are being quoted a 30-year fixed rate mortgage in which your payments will never change, have him show you where it says this and ask him to put it in writing. *(You can also determine this by reviewing your Truth In Lending disclosure that the planner is required to give you by law and that you will sign. Simply look at the itemization of payments; if they change, then you are in an ARM).*

6. If you are in a low teaser rate mortgage, have your planner indicate when the first change date will occur and ask her to indicate what rate the adjustment might go to. *(Review your ARM and your Truth In Lending disclosures. These will detail worst the case scenario).*

7. Is there a pre-payment penalty and if yes, how does it work? Have your mortgage planner put it in writing. If no, also have him put it in writing. *(If there is a pre-payment penalty, laws require that this be disclosed on a separate form that you will sign).*

8. If the rate sounds too good to be true, chances are that something will be different at the closing.

Although the process may seem confusing and there is a lot of paperwork, if you just *s l o w d o w n* and actually read all of the disclosures provided when you apply and again at the closing table there should not be any surprises and you will know exactly what you are signing up for.

If you would like a form containing the above questions to use with your planner, one can be obtained when you visit www.mortgageswhatyouneedtoknow.com.

Again the best place to find a mortgage planner is to ask your family, friends and other advisors who they used *and* whether they were happy. If that does not work and you are not sure where to find a good mortgage planner simply visit www.forgottenequity.com.

APPENDIX

TOP 10 MISTAKES YOU MAY HAVE MADE WITH YOUR CURRENT MORTGAGE

1. BOUGHT A HOUSE BEYOND YOUR MEANS

In today's society of keeping up with the Joneses, most of us buy a house much bigger than we really need. We do this to impress others or for our own ego. Purchasing a less expensive house saves tens of thousands of dollars of mortgage payments and utility bills that can be re-directed toward long term planning such as retirement and college funding.

2. WAITED UNTIL THE LAST MINUTE TO APPLY

Like everything else in life, if you waited until the last minute to apply for a mortgage, you did not give yourself enough time to research and *ensure* that you got the best program for your family. When purchasing a home, you should start the process with your mortgage planner—not the realtor. After you have analyzed your goals, dreams and finances you then enlist a realtor with a mortgage plan in hand to help you find your home.

Your realtor will also appreciate this; she will know that you are qualified to be looking at the price point you requested. By doing it the other way around *(as most people do)*, you were rushed into a home-buying decision and acted out of impulse or emotion, and not from sound thinking. On refinance transactions you waited until you could no longer pay your bills or late notices were pilling up. If you implement a review (see item 5, below) below and further detailed in Chapter Sixteen, you can take control of your financial future.

3. Took out a 30-Year Fixed Rate Mortgage

The national average for time we stay in our homes is seven years. The national average for a mortgage is 4.2 years. Yet you still took out a 30-year mortgage. If you shorten the term of your mortgage to an Adjustable Rate Mortgage (ARM) you can create additional cash flow to invest toward long term growth. The <u>*key*</u> here is to invest the difference of what your 30-year fixed rate mortgage costs, versus what your payments would be with an ARM. This is how you build wealth! Chapter Seven details the questions you must ask yourself before taking out any mortgage.

4. Paying down the Principal Balance of Your Loan

Money you pay towards the principal balance is money you will never see again unless you sell or refinance. Furthermore, equity in your home has a *zero* rate of return. In addition, each payment you make reduces your tax deductions; exposes you to greater risk of liability and market downturns; reduces your chances of qualifying for financial aid for college tuition; provides you with less liquidity and reduces money that could have gone to other investments.

5. Failing to Review Your Mortgage *Every Year*

Life happens! Your circumstances can change each year. One spouse may have stopped working or went back to work. You may have gotten injured or possibly laid off and run up some debt. Your credit scores may have improved, opening up better programs that might not have been available to you when you took out your current mortgage. Maybe you want to make improvements to your home? You have to pay for college? A Mortgage Check-Up can also help prevent identity theft through a credit check. Chapter Sixteen details why this is so important and how you will benefit.

6. FIGURING RATE WAS THE MOST IMPORTANT FEATURE

This is one of the most common misconceptions people make when looking for a new mortgage. Rate is not the most important feature, the monthly payment and right program are. Yes, rate determines the payment, but *how you structure* your mortgage will have a greater impact on your overall financial success, more than the rate will. You could have a great rate but be in the wrong program and that could cost you thousands of dollars that would otherwise be invested towards your future.

7. STICKING TO THE I'M-DOING-OKAY-SO-WHY-DO-SOMETHING-NONTRADITIONAL ATTITUDE

Even if you are doing okay, the question is: by who's standards? Don't rationalize where you are. Even if you are doing great by properly structuring your mortgage, you can do even better. If you are not where you want to be then you *should* look at alternatives. The goal is to have a very rich retirement. Using a mortgage correctly can turbo charge your lifestyle during the retirement years.

8. BEING TOO BUSY TO CONSIDER ALTERNATIVES, OR, USING THE I'LL-WORRY- ABOUT-THAT LATER REFRAIN

Most Americans spend more time planning their family vacation than their financial future. What you are really saying is that you don't want to learn anything new. Or, you are financially embarrassed about where you are today so the less you talk about it the better you will feel. *This is why* 90% of Americans today will not be able to retire. *This is why* the average 45-year-old only has $27,000 set aside in retirement accounts. *This is why* we as a country have a negative savings rate. This means we are spending more than we make.

9. Making a Large Down Payment

Perhaps this should have been the number two choice, but most people think a large down payment will save money over the length of the mortgage. But the more you put down, the less you have creating wealth in other investments, in addition to the pitfalls detailed in item number 4, above, and Chapter Five.

10. Figuring It's *Just* a Mortgage

A mortgage today is more than just a mortgage. Today we see a mortgage as a financial instrument that should be tied to both short and long term financial goals. The type of mortgage you have dramatically affects your net worth and directly impacts your ability to retire! Advanced Mortgage Planning Strategies can help you use your mortgage to create wealth and peace of mind!

Six Things You Should Do Right Away

1. Visit www.optoutprescreen.com and opt yourself out of the trigger lists.

2. Wait at least three business days and then run and review your credit at www.annualcreditreport.com to check for any false information that could negatively affect you.

3. Conduct an annual review with the form provided. Review your current situation. If you think you can improve upon it, contact a mortgage planner to see how a professional would advise you.

4. Take out a Home Equity Line of Credit as a life jacket. Do this if your review suggests you are okay or after you refinance based upon the advice from your planner.

5. Build your liquid reserve account of six months in case Life Happens!

6. Visit www.mortgageswhatyouneedtoknow.com for free forms mentioned in this book as well as other materials and information.

Mortgage Check-Up Form

Use this section ONLY if you plan on sending this form to your Mortgage Planner in advance of your review.

First Name: ______________________ Last Name: ______________________

Spouse First Name: _________________ Spouse Last Name: _________________

Address: ____________________________________ Town: ___________________

State: ____________ Zip Code: ______________

Your email: ______________________ Spouse's email: ________________________

Best time to contact you __________ at what number? (c) (h) (w) ___________________

Property Information Section
(complete one for each property you have)

The questions in this section are to help your Mortgage Planner get a head start on determining if he/she can **HELP YOU**. Please complete the information below to the best of your knowledge. If you don't know all of it you can review with your planner.

1. What **type** of mortgage do you currently have? ________________ (30-year fixed or an ARM) Interest Only? Yes No
2. What is your loan balance? $_____________ What is your current interest rate? ________
3. What is your current mortgage payment, principal and interest only? $ _____________ This figure should not include your property taxes, insurance and/or any association dues.
4. Property Taxes: $ __________/YR Insurance: $ ________/YR Dues? $ ______/Month
5. Do you have a 2nd Mortgage or a Line of Credit? If yes, what is your current balance $ _________ Your interest rate ________ and your monthly payment $ _________ Interest Only? Yes No
6. Circle your type of home: Single Family 2-Family 3-Family 4-Family Condo Townhouse Co-Op
7. If you were to list your house for sale **today** what is it worth? $________________
8. Total credit card debt $____________ and the combined monthly minimum payment $_______
9. What is your credit score _________ and your spouse's ___________

Depending upon the information you completed above, you may be able to benefit from a refinance transaction to improve upon your current program, consolidate debts and/or possible repositioning of some home equity towards college and/or retirement planning. For a larger form to print and use please visit www.mortgageswhatyouneedtoknow.com.

Glossary

Language you need to know:

Adjustable Rate Mortgage (ARM)

An ARM mortgage is one in which the interest rate and payments are not fixed and are subject to change at prescribed dates.

Amortized Loan

An amortized loan is one in which each payment consists of both principal and interest; each month your loan balance gets reduced.

Amortization

Amortization is the process of gradual payment of a debt through regular installments that cover both interest and principal.

Annual Percentage Rate (APR)

APR is the rate used to compare loan choices by factoring in all of the banks costs associated with the loan.

Appraisal

An appraisal is an expert and unbiased opinion of the value or worth of a property.

Arbitrage

Arbitrage is a method of attempting to profit by exploiting price differences of identical or similar financial instruments by buying and selling them on different markets or in different forms.

BALLOON MORTGAGE

A balloon mortgage is one in which the entire principal balance is due in a lump sum at a pre-determined date, which is earlier than the date that it would become due under a normal, amortization schedule.

BASIS POINT

A basis point is one hundredth of a percent (0.01%). It is used to measure changes in or differences between yields or interest rates.

CAPS (INTEREST)

CAPs relating to interest are consumer safeguards that limit the extent to which the interest rate on an adjustable rate mortgage may change per year and/or during the life of the loan.

CAPS (PAYMENT)

CAPs relating to payment are consumer safeguards that limit the extent to which monthly payments on an adjustable rate mortgage may change.

CASH-OUT REFINANCE

A cash-out refinancing is a transaction in which the money the borrower receives from the new loan exceeds the total amount he uses to repay the existing first mortgage and closing costs. In other words, it is a refinance transaction in which the borrower receives additional cash he can use for any purpose.

CASH FLOW

Cash flow refers to a measure of financial health; it equals your monthly income minus your total expenses.

COMPOUND INTEREST

Compound interest is interest that is calculated not only on the initial principal but also the accumulated interest of prior periods.

COMPOUNDING

Compounding is a process whereby the value of an investment increases exponentially over time due to compound interest. Interest earned in one period, for example, earns additional interest during each subsequent time period.

CONFORMING LOAN AMOUNT

A conforming loan amount is a loan that is at or below the amount set for jumbo programs. As of the date of writing, the conforming loan amount was set at $417,000 and below.

CONSUMER PRICE INDEX (CPI)

CPI is an inflationary indicator that measures the change in the cost of a fixed basket of products and services including housing, electricity, food, and transportation. The CPI is published monthly and is sometimes referred to as the cost-of-living index.

CONVENTIONAL MORTGAGE

A conventional mortgage is a loan arranged between lender and borrower with no government guarantee or insurance.

DEBT-TO-INCOME (DTI) FRONT

DTI (front) refers to total housing expenses on a refinance (anticipated housing expenses on a purchase), divided by your gross monthly income.

DEBT-TO-INCOME (DTI) BACK

DTI (back) refers to total housing expenses on a refinance (anticipated housing expenses on a purchase) plus ALL of your other monthly expenses as they appear on your credit report or as they appear on your tax returns, divided by your gross monthly income.

Deferred Interest

Deferred interest is interest that is paid at a later date. By paying less than the actual amount of interest due on a loan, the shortfall is added to your loan balance.

Home Equity

Home equity is the value of a property, minus the outstanding mortgage balance(s).

Home Equity Line of Credit (HELOC)

A HELOC is a loan in which you are approved for a certain amount of money but no payments are due until you actually draw from the account via a checkbook the lender provides.

Federal Home Loan Mortgage Corporation (FHLMC) (Freddie Mac)

Freddie Mac is a federal-government-chartered corporation that buys qualified mortgage loans from the financial institutions that originate them. Freddie Mac then securitizes the loans and distributes the securities through the dealer community. The securities are not backed by the U.S. government. The market value of these securities prior to maturity is not guaranteed and will fluctuate.

Federal National Mortgage Association (FNMA) (Fannie Mae)

Fannie Mae is a Congressionally chartered corporation that buys mortgages on the secondary market, pools them and sells them as mortgage-backed securities to investors on the open market. Monthly principal and interest payments are guaranteed by Fannie Mae, but not by the U.S. government.

Fixed-Rate Mortgage

With a fixed-rate mortgage, interest rates remain the same over the life of the loan.

Good Faith Estimate (GFE)

A good faith estimate is a form provided by your lender as required by law to itemize all of your closing costs for the loan.

HUD-1 Settlement

A HUD-1 Settlement Statement, provided to you at the closing of mortgage (purchase or refinance) details all expenses and fees in connection with a real estate closing. The expenses will include your bank fees, escrows, closing agent fees as well as any monies exchanged between the buyer and the seller.

Index

An index is a published interest rate against which lenders measure the difference between the current interest rate on an adjustable rate mortgage and that earned by other investments (e.g. one, three, and five-year U.S. Treasury Security yields, monthly average interest rates on loans closed by S&Ls, and the monthly average Costs-of-Funds incurred by S&Ls). That figure is then used to adjust the interest rate on an adjustable mortgage up or down.

Interest

Interest refers to the cost of borrowing money, usually expressed as a percentage over time or the amount earned on an investment.

Interest Only Loan

An interest only loan is a non-amortized loan in which interest is due at regular intervals until maturity, when the full principal on the loan is due or until it converts to an amortized loan requiring both interest and principal payments.

Interest Rate Ceiling

The interest rate ceiling is the highest interest rate possible under an ARM. You may hear this called the lifetime CAP and it based on the number of percentage points your rate can increase from your initial rate.

Interest Rate Increase Cap

The interest rate increase CAP is the maximum allowable increase in your interest rate (on an ARM) each time your rate is adjusted. It is usually 1 or 2 percentage points. For example, if your rate adjusts every year, each year it cannot exceed the stated CAP.

Interest Rate Index

The interest rate index is the specific fund/security to which the interest rate on your ARM mortgage is tied. Common indexes are Treasury Constant Maturities or Cost of Funds indexes. All the indexes are published regularly in readily available sources such as newspapers.

Jumbo Mortgage

A jumbo mortgage loan is above the amount set for conforming programs. As of the date of writing it was set at $417,001 and above.

Liquidity

Liquidity is the ability of an asset to be converted into cash quickly, usually within 24 hours.

Loan-to-Value Ratio (LTV)

LTV is the relationship between the amount of the mortgage loan and the appraised value of the property expressed as a percentage.

Lender Paid Private Mortgage Insurance (LPMI)

Lender paid private mortgage insurance is required when you have a down payment or home equity of less than 20%. The premium is based on the loan amount and is factored into your interest rate.

Margin

A margin is the amount a lender adds to the index on an adjustable rate mortgage to establish the adjusted interest rate.

Mortgage

A mortgage is the claim by a lender against property until the debt is paid.

Mortgage (Late)

A mortgage payment that is received by the lender 30 days past its due date is late.

Negative Amortization

Negative amortization occurs when your monthly payments are not large enough to pay all the interest due on the loan. This unpaid interest is added to the unpaid principal balance of the loan. The danger of negative amortization is that the borrower ends up owing more than the original amount of the loan.

Option ARM

An option ARM is a complicated mortgage that provides several different types of mortgage payments each month. It is meant to be used by financially savvy clients.

Opportunity Cost

The phrase "opportunity cost" means that by tying your money up in a particular way, you miss the chance to invest your dollars elsewhere in an investment that, in theory, would have provided you with a better rate of return.

Per Diem Interest

Per diem interest is the daily cost of borrowed money from a lender.

PITI

PITI equals the principal, interest, taxes, and insurance, forming the basis for monthly mortgage payments.

Private Mortgage Insurance (PMI)

PMI is required when you have a down payment or home equity of less than 20%. The premium is based on the loan amount.

Prepayment Penalty

A prepayment penalty is a charge sometimes imposed on a borrower who prepays his mortgage (that is, pays it off before the maturity date).

Rate of Return

Rate of return is the annual return on an investment, expressed as a percentage of the total amount invested.

Refinancing

Refinancing is applying for a new mortgage on your existing home.

Tax Deferral

Tax deferral is the act of delaying tax liability until some future date. For individuals this may be done by making investments such as IRA, 401(k), SEP IRA, or Keogh plans, where taxes are paid when funds are withdrawn. For a business entity, this may be achieved by taking accelerated depreciation of assets, which can result in the delay of tax liabilities.

Truth in Lending Disclosure

The Truth in Lending Disclosure form provides information set forth by federal law to give you information about the costs of your loan so that you may compare programs or lenders.

References:

To check your credit report:

- ✓ www.annualcreditreport.com

To remove your name from trigger lists:

- ✓ www.optoutprescreen.com

For additional resources about the opt-out process can be found at The Federal Trade Commission's Prescreening Information Pamphlet.

- ✓ www.ftc.gov/bcp/conline/pubs/credit/prescreen.pdf

To learn about tax deductibility of mortgage interest and points and to obtain IRS Publication 936:

- ✓ www.irs.gov/publications/p936/index.htm

To learn more about taxes and mortgage points (IRS Topic 504 - Home Mortgage Points):

- ✓ www.irs.gov/taxtopics/tc504.html

For a good explanation on the TIL and APR:

- ✓ www.in.gov/dfi/education/questions_and_answers_til.htm

To find a good mortgage planner:

- ✓ Ask your friends if they liked theirs
- ✓ www.forgottenequity.com

For more free forms and other materials:

- ✓ www.mortgageswhatyouneedtoknow.com

About the Author

David A. Muti, JD, RMA, is a Senior Mortgage Planner with **Millenium Home Mortgage, LLC** based in New Jersey. In this role he manages a team of specialists who assist clients in the purchase and refinancing of homes and investment properties. Dave meets with clients daily educating them on alternative methods of leverage and retirement planning, enabling families to obtain their dreams and goals of home ownership and asset protection for a safer and happier retirement. He teaches his clients how to make money using their mortgage as a financial instrument. This is accomplished by structuring their home financing in a manner that will achieve the goals of maximizing tax deductions, improving their current cash flow, increasing their net worth and ultimately increasing their retirement income. In addition to his role with clients, Mr. Muti is a founding member and president of Forgotten Equity, Inc. Here he leads the vision and strategic growth of the company which serves as an online sales and marketing firm for individuals specializing in the mortgage and financial planning industries through its proprietary software. The company's mission is to educate the consumer while serving as the marketplace for these two industries to work in tandem to preserve consumers' assets and grow their overall wealth to a level they never thought possible.

Mr. Muti is a seasoned professional with extensive profit-and-loss, operational and general management experience. His background is deeply entrenched in real estate, beginning in college with the purchase of his first home and then with the establishment of his law practice in 1991-2000. He has a proven track record of successfully building and advising profitable new businesses and improving established businesses. Previously, Mr. Muti was a manager of international real estate at a Fortune 500 company overseeing leasehold acquisitions in Europe and Asia. Before that Mr. Muti was a partner in a general practice law firm that concentrated on real estate and small business needs. In November 2007 Dave stepped down from the Board of

Directors of Chronic Disease Fund, Inc., a national charity based out of Frisco, Texas to focus on writing and his clients. CDFund.org is one of the largest providers of co-pay assistance for chronic disease in the country, providing financial assistance to those underinsured patients diagnosed with chronic or life altering diseases and need expensive, specialty therapeutics. Mr. Muti is a graduate of Ithaca College and Vermont Law School and has lived in Morris County, New Jersey since 1977. He has a beautiful wife and has two sons.

Endorsements and Praise

Finally, someone has compiled a thorough yet easy to understand reference manual that has everything you need to know to optimize your real estate investments. This book is not about selling you something. It is about educating you. Avoid the grief of ignorance and implement the strategies to take control of your financial future.

-Lee M. Brower, Featured Teacher from The Secret and Founder of Empowered Wealth/Quadrant Living Experience, UT

"Mortgages, What You Need to Know" is about a lot more than making those monthly payments to the bank. Mr. Muti, a mortgage authority, makes this mundane subject not only readable, but useful. As he rightly points out, a mortgage is often one of the most important financial decisions a person makes. That being said, it's amazing how flippant many have been this past decade when it comes to home finance. This casual attitude toward borrowing against one's home is largely to blame for the latest credit crunch. If only more people had read a book like this one. Know anyone contemplating buying their first home? Wondering about which is the best mortgage strategy for you to pursue to get that vacation home? Your first step should be to read this book.

-Joseph Finora Jr., Southampton Press, NY

This book breaks down the basics so the average consumer will have a better understanding of what their mortgage is and more importantly how to use the information to benefit their financial future. I see how this book can become a nice value add for financial professionals to use with their clients in connection with their services. Great Job!

-Steven Marshall, CEO, Strategic Equity and Founder of Mortgage Planner Magazine, WA

Finally! A How to Book on how to understand the mortgage process. After reading the book it made so much sense that anyone wanting to own a home or anyone in the mortgage business should read this book. It will not only educate you on the process but it will give you the edge you need especially in this market. This is a must read and it's on my recommended reading list. If you are a mortgage professional this book is a great resource to give to your clients to help better educate them in conjunction with your services.

-Matt De La Cruz, Founder and CEO of The Winning Minds Group, MI

If you own a house, you need this book! The financially savvy homeowner will benefit from the tools to increase cash-flow and maximize wealth. This book should be part of every Financial Planner's library.

-Diane K. Taylor, CFP®, EA, Past President - Financial Planning Association of New Jersey

As a matrimonial attorney handling divorce matters, my clients are often faced with having to refinance a home or assume a mortgage on a new home. This book offers valuable information and is presented in a manner that is easy to comprehend. It particularly helps my clients better understand how a mortgage impacts their future financially and alleviates some of their financial uncertainty. The advice and explanations provided assist both attorneys and their clients in order to make sound financial decisions based upon logic and reason.

-Debra S. Weisberg, Esq., Donahue, Hagan, Klein, Newsome & O'Donnell, P.C., NJ

A great prelude for anyone remotely interested in exploring mortgage planning strategies. A must read for the consumer and both the rookie and seasoned mortgage professional... a powerful and critical foundation for productive planning sessions.

-Paul W. Haarman, CEO & Co-Founder Renaissance Mortgage Corporation, NH

We spend a lot of time educating people about mortgages and this book has become part of our process to raise the level of our clients' knowledge and our conversation. Better educated clients allow us more quality time to help to determine the right mortgage for their future. This small investment in knowledge will more than quadruple the return for our clients and our firm. This book is a must read; where was it 3 or 4 years ago...

-Albert J. Perkins, IV, Founder and CEO, CNRG Corp., HI

The information in this book is must read for 1st Time Home Buyers. I would also encourage all bankers and brokers to have all Loan Officers read this as part of their training curriculum. This book does a great job of breaking down mortgage financing into simple terms!

-Jon Lamkin, Senior VP, Northern Region, Financial Resources, NJ

As a best selling author of personal finance books and a 20-year veteran of the mortgage industry, I understand the value of shining the light of knowledge on your path of life. This book can be a flashlight, illuminating your obstacles and road signs, guiding you to more rewarding choices. Instead of just blindly following the guy in front of you or the old paths you stumble upon that leave you wandering in financial circles, grab this guide and put on your shades as you view your sunny future.

-Marian Snow Author of Stop Sitting On Your Assets, MO

As a Certified Financial Planner I have been advising clients for over 15 years about mortgages. Most clients believe mortgages are simple to understand and who ever has the lowest rate wins. But there are lots of hidden "gotchya's". This book discusses the real issues and puts you, the consumer, back in the driver seat. I enjoyed reading it and learned a few things myself. Finally a mortgage book that makes cents!

-Richard Brownstein, CFP®, Founder and President, Financial Health Center, NJ

This book is an asset for our clients and our firm. It takes the mortgage process; clarifies and simplifies it, then lays the foundation for strategic mortgage planning in a way that it is understandable and not overwhelming. We plan to get this in the hands of each of our clients prior to our first meeting.

-Chad Orstad, CRMS, CMP, CMPS, President & Co-Founder, T.N.T. Mortgage, Inc., MO

What an amazing tool! This book blew my mind as to how well it makes complicated issues, simple & easy to understand. For any manager or originator, this would be a phenomenal tool to train you & your team on how to help clients make better mortgage decisions. I also love the consumer focus of the book, for the first time the industry now has a tool that really helps clients understand the basics of a mortgage, but at the same time clarifies what the long term impact of those decisions will be on their financial future. Dave, I especially love how willing you are to freely give the consumer several additional tools that will help consumers make better mortgage choices! Truly, thank you for providing exactly what the industry needs right now!

-Erik A. Janeczko, Coach/Coach Instructor, Maximum Acceleration, The LoanToolbox Coaching Company™, MO

As a TV host and a Certified Financial Planner® practitioner for over 20 years, this book has taught me several new strategies to help improve the financial outlook for my clients. Thank you for sharing this valuable information!

-Saul M. Simon CFP®, CFS, RFC, Private Wealth Advisor, Simon Financial Group, NJ

A must read for anyone who has a mortgage or is thinking about buying a home.

-Allan D. Koltin, CPA, President & CEO, PDI Global, Inc., IL

As a professional who works with clients on optimizing all of their financial assets, this book is an excellent resource for first time homebuyers and seasoned real estate investors.

-Gary R. Scheer, CSA, Radio Talk Show Host, Founder Financial Management Group, NJ

Dave Muti is a leading authority on Mortgages and this book is an outstanding must-read primer for anyone who works with, owns or is thinking of owning residential real estate. This book reveals the inside secrets on how these incredibly important financial products are created, marketed, and used in easy to understand language. From sophisticated financial advisors to current and prospective homeowners, this book will take you on an eye opening journey through the details and strategies that you need to know.

-Kaushal "Ken" Majmudar, JD, CFA, President and Chief Investment Officer, The Ridgewood Group, NJ

To quote Leonard Renier -*Knowledge is power. Knowledge can be time-consuming and expensive. Now, consider the cost of not knowing something. There lieth the lesson.* This book is a compass to help guide and educate clients as well as advisors through the maze of what is to be the largest financial decision they or their clients will ever make. This has to be in the hands of those that plan on purchasing or refinancing. Whether you are a first time home buyer, a seasoned real estate investor or a financial professional using this with your clients, you will walk away with knowledge that you can use right away to improve your situation.

-Robin Barnes, LifePro Financial Services, Inc, Founder/President Educational Institute of the Southwest, CA

Notes

Notes

Notes

Notes